THROUGHPUT ACCOUNTING

A GUIDE TO CONSTRAINT MANAGEMENT

THROUGHPUT ACCOUNTING

A GUIDE TO CONSTRAINT MANAGEMENT

STEVEN M. BRAGG

JOHN WILEY & SONS, INC.

Library of Congress Cataloging-in-Publication Data:

Bragg, Steven M.
  Throughput accounting : a guide to constraint management / Steven M. Bragg.
    p. cm.
  ISBN-13: 978-0-471-25109-5 (cloth)
  1. Theory of constraints (Management)   2. Productivity accounting.   I. Title.
  HD69.T46B73 2007
  658.5′036–dc22

                                                        2006032738

10 9 8 7 6 5 4 3 2 1

To the production crew at John Wiley, who might know a thing or two about bottlenecks—usually the authors!

CONTENTS

About The Author

Steven Bragg, CPA, CMA, CIA, CPIM, has been the chief financial officer or controller of four companies, as well as a consulting manager at Ernst & Young and auditor at Deloitte & Touche. He received a master's degree in finance from Bentley College, an MBA from Babson College, and a bachelor's degree in Economics from the University of Maine. He has been the two-time president of the Colorado Mountain Club, and is an avid alpine skier, mountain biker, and certified master diver. Mr. Bragg resides in Centennial, Colorado. He has written the following books, published by John Wiley & Sons:

Accounting and Finance for Your Small Business
Accounting Best Practices
Accounting Control Best Practices
Accounting Reference Desktop
Billing and Collections Best Practices
Business Ratios and Formulas
The Controller's Function
Controller's Guide to Costing
Controller's Guide to Planning and Controlling Operations
Controller's Guide: Roles and Responsibilities for the New Controller
Controllership
Cost Accounting
Design and Maintenance of Accounting Manuals
Essentials of Payroll
Fast Close
Financial Analysis
GAAP Guide
GAAP Implementation Guide
Inventory Accounting
Inventory Best Practices
Just-in-Time Accounting

Managing Explosive Corporate Growth
The New CFO Financial Leadership Manual
Outsourcing
Payroll Accounting
Payroll Best Practices
Revenue Recognition
Sales and Operations for Your Small Business
The Ultimate Accountants' Reference

Other books authored by Mr. Bragg include:
Advanced Accounting Systems (Institute of Internal Auditors)
Run the Rockies (CMC Press)

FREE ON-LINE RESOURCES BY STEVE BRAGG

Steve Bragg issues a free bi-monthly accounting best practices newsletter and an accounting best practices podcast. You can sign up for both at www.stevebragg.com.

PREFACE

The practice of throughput accounting is about how to wring more profits from your company by focusing strictly on the management of your bottleneck resource, or constraint. This approach is entirely at odds with the traditional use of detailed allocations to arrive at fully burdened costs for your products, customers, and sales regions—which can yield results so convoluted that a company can become paralyzed with indecision. Not so with throughput accounting, which yields crisp and easy to understand results for a broad range of management applications.

Throughput Accounting begins with an introduction to the concepts of constraint management, followed by supplemental information about how it is used in the factory for daily production decisions. The book then addresses how constraint management can be applied within the accounting department, beginning with a comparison between it and other cost accounting systems. Of particular interest are two chapters on financial analysis scenarios and case studies that show specifically how throughput accounting can be used to find the best solutions in a large number of real-world situations.

Throughput Accounting also explores how the traditional budgeting and capital budgeting models can be adapted to integrate throughput concepts, as well as how control systems can be designed to warn of problems related to the constraint and several supporting functions. In addition, the book shows which reports and metrics to use in a throughput environment, as well as how this information can be extracted from an accounting system designed to accumulate information for reports that conform to generally accepted accounting principles.

If you are an accounting manager, financial analyst, production planner, or production manager, then *Throughput Accounting* contains the tools you need to improve your companys performance.

STEVEN M. BRAGG
Centennial, Colorado
September 2006

1

OVERVIEW OF THE THEORY
OF CONSTRAINTS

Every now and then, a completely new idea comes along that can be described as either refreshing, disturbing, or both. Within the accounting profession, the theory of constraints is that change. It originated in the 1980s through the writings of Eliyahu Goldratt. His training as a physicist, rather than as an accountant, appears to have given him a sufficiently different mind-set to derive several startling changes to the concepts of operational enhancement and cost accounting. The theory of constraints is based on the concept that a company must determine its overriding goal, and then create a system that clearly defines the main capacity constraint that will allow it to maximize that goal. This chapter describes the operational and financial aspects of the theory of constraints.

DEFINITIONS FOR THE OPERATIONAL ASPECTS
OF THE THEORY OF CONSTRAINTS

Comprehending the operational aspects of the theory of constraints requires some understanding of a new set of terms that are not used in traditional company operations. The terms are as follows:

- *Drum.* This is the element in a company's operations that prevents the company from producing additional sales. This is the company's constrained capacity resource or bottleneck operation. It will most likely be a machine or person, though it also might

1

be a short supply of materials. Because total company results are constrained by this resource, it beats the cadence for the entire operation—in essence, it is the corporate drum.

- *Buffer.* The drum operation must operate at maximum efficiency in order to maximize company sales. However, it is subject to the vagaries of upstream problems that impact its rate of production. For example, if the drum is located in the production department, then if the stream of work-in-process generated by an upstream work center is stopped, the inflow of parts to the drum operation will cease, thereby halting sales. To avoid this problem, it is necessary to build a buffer of inventory in front of the drum operation to ensure that it will continue operating even if there are variations in the level of production created by feeder operations. The size of this buffer will be quite large if the variability of upstream production is large, and correspondingly smaller if the upstream production variability is reduced.

- *Rope.* This term refers to the timed release of raw materials into the production process to ensure that a job reaches the inventory buffer before the drum operation is scheduled to work on it. In essence, the rope is the synchronization mechanism driving the flow of materials to the drum operation. The length of the rope is the time required to keep the inventory buffer full, plus the processing time required by all operations upstream of the drum operation.

These three terms are frequently clustered together to describe the theory of constraints as the drum-buffer-rope (DBR) system. The following section discusses the mechanics of the DBR system.

THE OPERATIONAL ASPECTS OF THE THEORY OF CONSTRAINTS

Pareto analysis holds that 20 percent of events cause 80 percent of the results. For example, 20 percent of customers generate 80 percent of all profits, or 20 percent of all production issues cause 80 percent of the scrap. The theory of constraints, when reduced down to one guiding concept, states that one percent of all events cause 99 percent of the results. This conclusion is reached by viewing a company as one

Scenario One:

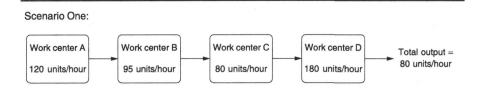

Scenario Two:

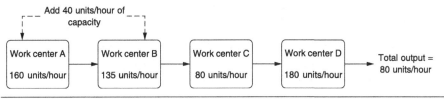

EXHIBIT 1.1   IMPACT OF THE DRUM OPERATION ON TOTAL OUTPUT

giant system designed to produce profits, with one bottleneck operation controlling the amount of those profits.

Under the theory of constraints, all management activities are centered on management of the bottleneck operation, or drum. By focusing on making the drum more efficient and ensuring that all other company resources are oriented toward supporting the drum, a company will maximize its profits. The concept is shown in Exhibit 1.1, where the total production capacity of four work centers is shown, both before and after a series of efficiency improvements are made. Of the four work centers, the capacity of center "C" is the lowest, at 80 units per hour. Despite subsequent efficiency improvements to work centers "A" and "B," the total output of the system remains at 80 units per hour, because of the restriction imposed by work center "C."

This approach is substantially different from the traditional management technique of local optimization, where *all* company operations are to be made as efficient as possible, with machines and employees maximizing their work efforts at all times.

The key difference between the two methodologies is the view of efficiency—should it be maximized everywhere, or just at the drum? The constraints-based approach holds that any local optimization of a non-drum resource will simply allow it to produce more than the drum operation can handle, which results in excess inventory. For example, a furniture company discovers that its drum operation is its paint shop. The company cannot produce more than 300 tables per day, because that maximizes the capacity of the paint shop. If the company adds a lathe to produce more table legs, this will only result in the accumulation of an excessive quantity of table legs, rather than the production of a larger number of painted tables. Thus, the investment in efficiencies elsewhere than the drum operation will only increase costs without improving sales or profits.

The preceding example shows that not only should efficiency improvements *not* be made in areas other than the drum operation, but that it is quite acceptable to not even be efficient in these other areas. It is better to stop work in a non-drum operation and idle its staff than to have it churn out more inventory than can be used by the drum operation.

Given the importance of focusing management attention on maximization of drum efficiencies, the use of buffers becomes extremely important. An inventory buffer should be positioned in front of the drum operation, and is used to provide a sufficient amount of stock to the drum to keep it running at maximum efficiency, even when variations in upstream work centers create short-term reductions in the flow of incoming inventory. The need for a buffer brings up a major operational concept in the theory of constraints, which is that there will be inevitable production failures that will alter the flow of inventory through the facility. Buffers are used to absorb the shock of these production failures, though it is also possible to increase the level of sprint capacity to offset the need for large buffers.

Sprint capacity is excess capacity built into a production operation that allows the facility to create excess inventory in the short term, usually to make up for sudden shortfalls in inventory levels. Sprint capacity is extremely useful for maintaining a sufficient flow of inventory into the drum operation, since the system can quickly recover from a production shortfall. If there is a great deal of sprint capacity in a production system, then there is less need for a buffer in front of the drum operation, since new inventory stocks can be generated quickly.

The concept of sprint capacity brings up an important point in the theory of constraints—that it is not only useful, but necessary to have excess capacity levels available in a system. This controverts the traditional management approach of eliminating excess capacity in order to reduce the costs associated with maintaining that capacity. Instead, management should be aware of those work centers with high levels of sprint capacity, which require much lower levels of inventory buffer, and primarily focus its attention on areas with low sprint capacity, which require larger buffer stocks.

Thus far, we have seen that the theory of constraints places a premium on maximum utilization of the drum operation, as well as the use of inventory buffers to support that utilization. One additional requirement is needed to ensure that the drum operates at maximum capacity at all times, which is the concept of the rope. The rope is the method used to release inventory into upstream production processes just in time to ensure that the drum operation and its buffer are fully supplied with the appropriate levels of work-in-process. If the rope releases inventory into the system too late, then the drum will be starved of input, and will produce less than its maximum amount. Conversely, the release of inventory too early will result in a large backlog of unfinished parts in front of the drum, which both represents an excessive investment in inventory and may result in confusion regarding which jobs to process next through the drum operation.

These factors comprise the drum-buffer-rope (DBR) elements of the theory of constraints, and will be explained more fully in Chapter 2, Constraint Management in the Factory. Having covered an overview of DBR, we will diverge briefly to address the nature of the constraint and then proceed to the financial aspects of the theory of constraints.

NATURE OF THE CONSTRAINT

The theory of constraints is based on the existence of a constraint, so it is useful to delve into the nature of this core concept. A constraint is a resource that limits a company's total output. For example, the constraint may be a machine that can only produce a specified amount of a key component in a given time period, thereby keeping overall sales from expanding beyond the maximum capacity of that machine. The key question to ask in locating this type of constraint is: "If we had more of it, could we generate more sales?" Physical constraints of this type tend to be easy to locate within a company because there is usually a large amount of work-in-process piled up in front of it, waiting to be processed.

The most common system constraint cannot be seen or touched—it is the operational policy. A policy is a rule that dictates how a system is operated. Examples of policies are batch sizing rules and resource utilization guidelines. For instance, a policy may state that a work station completely fill a pallet with work-in-process before sending it on to the next work station, since this makes it more efficient for the materials handling staff to move inventory through the factory. The trouble is that the next work station may be the constrained resource, which has to halt operations while waiting for the pallet to be filled. In this case, the policy should have allowed a more continuous flow of inventory to the constrained resource, which means that much smaller batch sizes would have improved the utilization of the constrained resource.

Policy constraints are usually difficult to find and eliminate. *Finding* them is difficult because policies are not physical entities that can be readily observed; instead, they must be deduced from the operational flow of the production system. *Eliminating* them can be even more difficult, since they may be strongly supported by employees, who require considerable convincing before agreeing to change a policy that they may have used for years. Though there may be considerable resistance to a policy change, the actual fix can be extremely inexpensive. Once eliminated, a policy constraint can result in a larger degree of system improvement than the elimination of any physical constraint.

A concept impacting the presence of policy constraints is the paradigm constraint. This is a belief that causes employees to follow a policy constraint. A classic paradigm constraint is the belief that every work center must be run at full tilt in order to increase its efficiency, which is a teaching of traditional cost accounting theory. However, this paradigm can result in a policy constraint to create a bonus plan that rewards factory managers for running all equipment at as close to 100 percent capacity as possible. The result is an excessive investment in inventory, and the divergence of resources away from the constrained resource. Thus, a paradigm constraint can be a powerful roadblock to the elimination of a policy constraint.

Another constraint may be a raw material, if there is not enough to ensure that all orders can be filled. This less common problem tends to arise during bursts of peak industry-wide sales, when materials suppliers are caught with insufficient production capacity to meet all demand (which means that the constraint has now shifted to the supplier!). This type of constraint will be immediately evident to the materials management staff, which cannot schedule jobs for release to the production area until sufficient materials are available.

Another possible constraint is the sales staff, if there are not enough people to bring in all possible customer orders. This constraint is evident when a large potential market or a significant number of sales prospects exist at the top of the sales funnel, but very few actual sales are being generated.

A company may improve its operations so much that its current capacity is able to handle all orders currently placed by customers. If so, the constraint has now shifted into the marketplace. The company must now use its higher capacity to offer better pricing deals or service levels to customers in order to increase its share of the market.

A company can also intentionally position a constraint on a specific resource. This happens when the capacity of a particular resource would be extremely expensive to increase, so managers prefer to focus their attention on maximizing the efficiency of the work center without actually adding capacity to it. It is also useful to avoid positioning the constraint on a resource that requires complex level of management, such as one where employee training or turnover levels are extremely high. Thus, the positioning of the constrained resource should be a management decision, rather than an accident.

DEFINITIONS FOR THE FINANCIAL ASPECTS OF THE THEORY OF CONSTRAINTS

To explain the financial aspects of the theory of constraints requires the use of several new terms (or old terms with new definitions), so we will define them first, before delving into the mechanics of the system. They are as follows:

- *Throughput.* The contribution margin that is left after a product's price is reduced by the amount of its totally variable costs (which is explained in the next bulleted point). There is no attempt to allocate overhead costs to a product, nor to assign to it any semi-variable costs. As a result, the amount of throughput for most products tends to be quite high.

- *Totally variable costs.* A cost that will only be incurred if a product is created. In many instances, this means that only direct materials are considered to be a totally variable cost, though subcontracting costs, commissions, customs duties, and transportation costs may also apply. Direct labor is not totally variable unless employees are only paid if a product is produced. The same rule applies to all other types of costs, so one will not find any type of overhead cost in the "totally variable cost" category.

- *Operating expenses.* The sum total of all company expenses, excluding totally variable expenses. Expenses usually categorized here are direct and indirect labor, depreciation, supplies, interest payments, and overhead. As a general rule, all expenses incurred as a result of the passage of time (rather than through the production process) are operating expenses. This group of expenses is considered to be the price a company pays to ensure that it maintains its current level of capacity. The theory of constraints does not care if a cost is semi-variable, fixed, or allocated—all costs that are not totally variable are lumped together into the Operating Expenses category.

- *Investment.* This definition is the same as one would find under standard accounting rules. However, there is a particular emphasis on a company's investment in working capital (especially inventory). The value of a company's investment in inventory does not include the value added by the system itself; so it does not include the value of direct labor or manufacturing overhead. The investment in inventory only includes amounts paid for components that are purchased from outside suppliers and used in the manufacture of inventory.

- *Net profit.* Throughput minus operating expenses.

These definitions are used to describe the financial aspects of the theory of constraints in the next two sections.

THE FINANCIAL ASPECTS OF THE THEORY OF CONSTRAINTS

The earlier discussion of the operational aspects of the theory of constraints might not appear to have a great deal of application to the work of the accountant, but its financial aspects reverse many long-standing principles of cost accounting. Since we are now covering an aspect of the theory of constraints that deals directly with the work of the accountant, we will refer to this area as throughput accounting.

A key concept of throughput accounting is the use of profitability analysis at the system level instead of gross margin analysis at the product level. In a traditional cost accounting system, costs from all parts of the production process are compiled and allocated by various means to specific products. When subtracted from product prices, this yields a gross margin that is used to determine whether a product is sufficiently profitable to be produced. Throughput accounting almost entirely ignores gross margin analysis at the product level. Instead, it considers the production process to be a single system whose overall profitability must be maximized.

The key reason for this difference in perspective is that most production costs do not vary directly with the incremental production of a single unit of a product. Instead, most production costs are required to maintain a system of production, irrespective of the number of product units created by it. For example, a traditional cost accounting system will assign the depreciation cost of a production machine to an overhead account, from which it is allocated by various means to each unit of a product manufactured. However, if one unit were not produced, would this result in a proportionate drop in the amount of overhead cost? Probably not. Instead, the same amount of overhead would now be assigned to the fewer remaining units produced, which raises their costs and lowers their gross profits.

To avoid this costing conundrum, throughput accounting uses an entirely different methodology, which is comprised of three elements: throughput, operating expenses, and investment. The key element of the three is throughput. To arrive at throughput, we subtract all *totally* variable costs from revenue. In reality, the only cost that varies totally with a product is the cost of its direct material. (Remember, even the cost of direct labor does not usually vary with the number of units produced.) In how many companies does the staff immediately go home when the last product is completed, or do employees get paid solely based on the number of units of production they create? Instead, the staff is employed on various other projects during downtime periods, to ensure that the same experienced staff is available for work the next day. The result of the throughput calculation is a very high level of throughput—much higher than a product's gross margin, which includes both labor and overhead costs.

The result of using throughput instead of gross margin is that hardly any products will *not* be produced due to a negative margin. This will only occur in a throughput accounting environment if a product's revenue is matched or exceeded by its raw material cost, which is rarely the case. Instead, products with a low throughput will still be included in the product mix, since they contribute to some degree to the total throughput of a company's production system.

The next element of throughput accounting is the concept of operating expenses. This category includes all other expenses besides the totally variable ones used to calculate throughput. Operating expenses are essentially all costs required to operate the production system. In throughput accounting, there is no distinction between totally fixed or partially fixed costs—again, they are either totally variable costs or part of operating expenses. By avoiding the considerable level of analysis required to deduce the variable elements of most largely fixed costs, financial analysis is greatly simplified, as will be seen in the multitude of examples in Chapter 4, Throughput and Financial Analysis Scenarios.

Throughput accounting also places considerable emphasis upon investment, which is the amount of money added to a system to improve its capacity. When combined with throughput, totally variable costs, and operating expenses, throughput accounting uses the following formulas for a wide array of accounting decisions:

Revenue − totally variable expenses = <u>throughput</u>

Throughput − operating expenses = <u>net profit</u>

Net profit/investment = <u>return on investment</u>

When making a decision involving changes to revenue, expenses, or investments, these three formulas can be used to arrive at the correct decision, which must yield a positive answer to one of the following three questions:

- Does it increase throughput?
- Does it reduce operating expenses?
- Does it improve the return on investment?

If a localized decision yields a positive answer to any one of these questions, then it will also improve the company-wide system, and so should be implemented.

When answering the three questions, it is best to favor decisions resulting in increased throughput, since there is potentially no upper limit to the amount of throughput that a company can generate. Decisions resulting in reduced operating expenses should be given the lowest action priority, since there is a limited amount of operating expense that can be reduced; also, a reduction of operating expenses may limit the production capacity of the system, which in turn may yield less throughput.

THE OPPORTUNITY COST OF OPERATIONS

A major concept of throughput accounting is to determine the true cost to a company of its capacity constraint. The capacity constraint is the drum operation, as described at the beginning of this chapter. If the use of the drum is not maximized, what is the opportunity cost to the company?

In a traditional cost accounting system, the cost would be the foregone gross margin on any products that could not be produced by the operation. For example, a work center experiences down time of one hour, because the machine operator is on a scheduled break. During that one hour, the work center could have created 20 products having a gross margin of $4.00 each. Traditional cost accounting tells us that this represents a loss of $80. Given this information, a manager might very well not back-fill the machine operator, and allow the machine to stay idle for the one-hour break period.

However, throughput accounting uses a different calculation of the cost of the capacity constraint. Since the performance of the constraint drives the total throughput of the entire system, the opportunity cost of not running that operation is actually the total operating expense of running the entire facility, divided by the number of hours during which the capacity constraint is being operated. This is because it is not possible to speed up the constrained operation, resulting in the permanent loss of any units that are not produced. For example, if the monthly operating expenses of a facility are $1.2 million and the constrained resource is run for every hour of that month, or 720 hours (30 days multiplied by 24 hours/day), then the cost per hour of the operation is $1,667 ($1,200,000 divided by 720 hours). Given this much higher cost of not running the operation, a manager will be much more likely to find a replacement operator for break periods.

What about the cost of not running a nonconstrained resource operation? As long as its downtime does not impact the operation of the constrained resource, it has no opportunity cost at all. In fact, the situation is reversed, for it is actually better to only run nonconstraint resources at the pace of the drum operation, since any excess inventory produced will only increase the amount of inventory in the production system—and this represents an additional investment in the system for which there is no offsetting increase in throughput.

Thus, there are substantial differences in the opportunity cost of running various operations, which can be interpreted differently with different accounting systems. Throughput accounting focuses attention on the high cost of not running a constrained resource, while showing that there is a negative opportunity cost associated with running a nonconstrained resource more than it is needed.

SUMMARY

This chapter was designed to give a general overview of the operational and financial underpinnings of the theory of constraints and throughput accounting. Here are the key issues covered so far:

- A company's results are largely driven by its management of a single constrained resource.

- The drum-buffer-rope system can be used to manage the constrained resource.
- Throughput accounting focuses on the total throughput of the system, rather than the gross margins of individual products.

In Chapter 2, we will expand upon the constraint management concept as it applies to a factory environment, and then devote the remainder of the book to an examination of a multitude of throughput accounting issues, including overhead allocation in Chapter 3, financial analysis in Chapter 4, budgeting and capital budgeting in Chapter 5, generally accepted accounting principles in Chapter 6, control systems in Chapter 7, performance measurement and reporting systems in Chapter 8, and accounting management issues in Chapter 9.

2

CONSTRAINT MANAGEMENT
IN THE FACTORY

We introduced the drum-buffer-rope concept in the first chapter as the best possible approach for managing a production process. This chapter delves into the details of each of these three areas, covering the following topics:

- *Drum (constraint).* How to locate the constraint, types of policy constraints, and management of the constraint
- *Buffer.* Components of the buffer and how to manage it
- *Rope.* The production scheduling task, as well as such ancillary topics as batch sizing and machine setups

This chapter is intended to give the reader a more in-depth understanding of constraint management in the factory, before we turn our attention in subsequent chapters to the financial aspects of constraint management.

LOCATING THE CONSTRAINT

Throughput accounting is centered on the total optimization of the constrained resource. However, in order to properly manage it, we must first locate this resource. It may not be immediately apparent, especially in a large production environment with many products, routings, and work centers. It is this "noise in the system" that prevents us from easily identifying constraints. Here are some questions to ask that will help locate it:

- *Where is there a work backlog?* If there is an area where work virtually never catches up with demand, where expeditors are constantly hovering, and where there are large quantities of inventory piled up, this is a likely constraint area.

- *Where do most problems originate?* Management usually finds itself hovering around a small number of work centers whose problems never seem to go away. Continuing problems are common at constrained resources, because they are so heavily utilized that there is never enough time to perform a sufficient level of maintenance, resulting in recurring breakdowns. In addition, there tends to be a fight over work priorities when there is not sufficient capacity, which also means that managers will be regularly called upon to determine these priorities among competing orders.

- *Where are the expediters?* An expediter physically steers a high-priority job through the production process. Because they frequently wait for available production time, their presence (especially several of them together) is a good indicator of a bottleneck.

- *Which work centers have high utilization?* Many companies measure the utilization level of their work centers. If so, review the list to determine which ones have a continually high level of utilization over multiple months. If a work center only briefly attains high utilization, it could still be the constraint if the reason for the lower utilization is ongoing maintenance problems or employee absenteeism.

- *What happens to total throughput when the constraint capacity changes?* If we add to the capacity of the suspected constraint, is there a noticeable increase in throughput? Conversely, if we deliberately reduce the capacity of the targeted work center (not recommended as a testing technique!), does overall throughput decline? If throughput does alter as a result of these changes, then we have probably located the constrained resource.

If, after this analysis, a company picks the wrong operation as its constrained resource, the real constraint will soon appear because of changes in the inventory buffers in front of the real and fake constraints. If the real constraint is upstream from the fake constraint, then the inventory buffer in front of the fake constraint will disappear.

This happens because management will focus its attention on improving the efficiency of the fake resource, thereby wiping out its backlog of work. The real constraint will be readily apparent, because it still has an inventory backlog. Conversely, if the real constraint is downstream from the fake constraint, then a larger inventory backlog will build in front of it. This happens because the same improvement in efficiency at the fake resource will result in a flood of additional inventory heading downstream, where it will dam up at the real constraint.

If products are engineered to order, then consider the engineering department to be part of the production process. This is important from the perspective of locating the constraint, because the constraint may not be in the traditional production area at all, but rather in the engineering department. Similarly, and for all types of product sales, the constraint may also reside in the sales department, where there may not be enough staff available to convert a large proportion of sales prospects into orders. This constraint is most evident when there are clearly many sales prospects at the top of the sales funnel, but there is a choke point somewhere in the sales conversion process, below which few orders are received. If this is the case, the solution is to enhance staffing for the sales positions specifically needed to improve handling of sales prospects at the choke point in the sales funnel.

Another constraint can also be raw materials. This problem arises during periods of excessive industry demand, resulting in materials allocations from suppliers. The location of this constraint will be immediately apparent to the materials management staff, which will have to reschedule production based on the shortage. However, this problem tends to be a short-term one, after which the constraint shifts back from the supplier and into the company.

It is also possible to designate a work center as the constrained resource. Taking this proactive approach is most useful when a work center requires a great deal of additional investment or highly skilled staffing to increase its capacity. By requiring that the constraint be focused on this area, management can profitably spend its time ensuring that the work center is fully utilized. It is also useful to avoid positioning the constraint on a resource that requires considerable management to operate properly, such as one where employee training or turnover levels are extremely high. Thus, positioning the constrained resource can be a management decision, rather than an incidental occurrence.

The pointers in this section are useful tools for locating a company's constrained resource. If not successfully located at once, a small number of iterations will soon cull out any "pretender" constraints, leaving the real constraint laid bare to a heightened level of management attention, as noted in the next section. Locating the constraint is the subject of one of the case studies in Chapter 10, Throughput Case Studies.

MANAGEMENT OF THE CONSTRAINED RESOURCE

If a company has a broad product mix that uses a wide array of work centers, it is entirely possible that there are multiple constrained resources. This is due to the fact that only a small proportion of total production is processed by each work center as the production mix shifts and the demand on key areas changes based on the unique features of current production needs. It is sometimes possible to restructure the factory into smaller focused sub-factories, for each of which there is a separate constrained resource. By taking this approach, it is easier to manage each of the constraints because of their greater visibility.

There are also situations where an upstream process is physically integrated into the constrained resource. This usually occurs when the industrial engineering staff thinks it can reduce labor costs by having machine operators manage more machines at the same time. However, though labor costs may be reduced, this will likely shrink throughput, since the extra number of tasks will interfere with the ability of the staff to manage the constrained resource. Thus, downtime at or extra effort required by the additional machines equates to downtime at the constraint. A better approach is to decouple the processes, so that the smallest number of operations are included in the constrained resource.

Once identified and isolated, management can use a number of ways to improve the throughput of the constrained resource. Several of the more common techniques are as follows:

- *Cover break time.* When employees stop a constrained resource to take a break from work, the company is suffering from the lost throughput that could have been generated during their break time. It is almost always cost-effective to pay someone else to work at the constraint during the work break, thereby gaining back capacity that would otherwise be gone for good. It is also possible to schedule the maintenance staff to work on the constraint during a break period; this especially makes sense when the maintenance staff would otherwise have to shut down the machine during a productive time period; combining two types of scheduled shutdown into one is an effective way to increase throughput.

- *Avoid downtime during shift changes.* A common occurrence is for a machine or work center to be shut down during a shift change, since outgoing employees like to spend a few minutes cleaning up their work areas before leaving, while incoming employees may require some time to review work schedules or attend meetings before they begin work. To avoid this downtime, consider having overlapping shifts, so that the incoming shift is on-site before the outgoing shift is scheduled to leave. This arrangement is only necessary for the constrained resource, not for other work centers that have excess capacity.

- *Offload incidental work.* If a machine operator is required to not only process materials at his workstation, but also to conduct maintenance and cleanup work, then there is a high likelihood that productive work will stop while the operator handles these additional tasks. This is a particular problem in companies where the maintenance department attempts to offload periodic minor maintenance onto the production staff; though this makes the job of the maintenance staff much easier, it can also reduce throughput! A better solution is to have an assistant handle all incidental work, thereby leaving the machine operator to ensure that the work center operates at maximum efficiency.

- *Replace equipment with staff.* In some cases, machines have replaced employees because of their higher processing speeds. However, employees may still be an alternative to the use of machines, since people can be more easily shifted in and out of constraint tasks. Thus, proper staff scheduling to handle work overloads at the constraint can result in a net increase in throughput.

- *Review for quality in front of the constraint.* The constrained resource only has a fixed amount of processing time available, so do not waste it by running materials through the constraint that already contain flaws that will lead to their rejection further in the manufacturing process. Instead, position a quality assurance person directly in front of the constraint, who is responsible for culling out any low-quality materials before they are used by the constrained resource.
- *Avoid rework at the constraint.* If the processing work at the constrained resource is not done properly, then materials must be routed back through this work center, which uses up valuable throughput time. To avoid it, have the industrial engineering staff closely examine the reasons why rework problems arise here and reduce their causes to a minimal level. This is an excellent area in which to practice total quality management (TQM) principles, where employees define a problem causing rework to occur, implement a solution, measure the solution's effectiveness, and then confirm and document their results in an iterative cycle of improvements.
- *Have backup staff available.* The operators of the constrained resource may not require the most extensive training (since this work center may not involve the most complex work in the facility), but it may still be a problem to locate replacements when the regular staff inevitably takes time off for a variety of reasons. To mitigate this issue, always have multiple, fully trained backup staff available. It may even be useful to give the backup employees regular training sessions, taught by the regular operators, just to ensure that they will operate at the highest possible level of efficiency when they are filling in for the regular staff. It is useful to pay a bonus to designated backup staff, to help ensure that there are enough volunteers available for this role.
- *Raise pay.* The best possible staffing should be used on the constrained resource. However, if the work is uninteresting, employees will be more likely to call in sick or transfer to other workstations. To ensure that the best possible staff is always

manning the constraint, offer the highest pay rate in the facility to those operators willing to work there.

- *Offload work to in-house work centers.* If there are other work centers in the production facility that can create products that are normally processed at the constrained resource—no matter how inefficient they may be—it will likely be cost-effective to shift some overflow work to these other work centers. By doing so, more throughput can be generated, while excess (and free) capacity at the other work centers can be utilized.

- *Outsource work.* If there are no opportunities to use the preceding recommendations to improve the throughput of in-house operations, then consider outsourcing some part of the production work to suppliers. As long as the throughput generated from this work exceeds its incremental outsourcing cost, then outsourcing is a viable option. Also, the supplier must be willing to invest in enough capacity to meet maximum demand levels, consistently make deliveries in time for the company to meet its customers' delivery dates, and ideally have the potential to grow beyond current production quantities as demand levels increase over time.

Use of the several of these techniques in order to manage a constraint is the subject of another case study in Chapter 10, Throughput Case Studies.

There are two other ways to manage the constrained resource, the use of proper inventory buffering and production scheduling (which are the *buffer-rope* elements of the *drum-buffer-rope* system described in Chapter 1). After a short diversion to address policy constraints, we will describe the proper management of buffers and production scheduling.

TYPES OF POLICY CONSTRAINTS

It was pointed out in the preceding chapter that a policy constraint is an extremely common problem that can reduce throughput levels. A policy is a rule that dictates how a system is operated, such as a *batch sizing rule* that a crate must be filled with work-in-process before being moved to the next downstream workstation. The trouble is that such a policy may keep materials from arriving at the downstream work-station in a timely manner. Consequently, the recipient workstation is starved of materials until the appropriate delivery crate is filled, and is then flooded with work when the crate arrives. Spotting the policy constraint in this example is relatively simple, because it results in downstream operations being alternatively flooded with materials or starved. This feast-famine cycle occurs because inventory builds up at an upstream workstation until a sufficient quantity has been completed to meet the policy guideline, triggering delivery of a large quantity to the downstream workstation.

Conversely, if an operation is continually starved of materials (but never flooded), then the constraint is likely to be caused by an upstream work center with inadequate capacity, rather than a policy.

There are a number of other common policy constraints. When they are mentioned in the following paragraphs, the name of each policy constraint will be italicized for easy reference. For example, a nego-tiated *break rule* that allows all machine operators a half-hour break period is a constraint when this means that no one is operating the con-strained resource during that half-hour period. In this case, the problem caused by the policy is obvious, but the solution may require painful labor negotiations to achieve. This problem arises for all types of *work rules,* which are frequently imposed by union agreements.

Another policy causing a constraint is the requirement to always have *production runs that do not drop below a set minimum level.* An excessively long production run creates too much inventory and also uses up valuable time at the constrained resource; thus, shorter pro-duction runs that only match immediate customer requirements are to be encouraged. This policy is usually engendered by a cost accounting analysis that points out that the cost of an expensive equipment setup can be reduced if spread over the cost of a great many units of pro-duction. However, since most work centers have excess capacity, the time required to make extra equipment setups for shorter production runs is actually free. This type of policy is discovered by investigating whether the scheduled amount of a production run matches demand, or if an excessive quantity has been scheduled by the production plan-ner. Another form of evidence is the presence of economic lot sizing rules where the computer recommends a lot size, rather than using the amount of actual customer orders. A secondary investigative approach is to review recent additions of finished goods to the warehouse and determine if they were added because of excess production.

Another type of policy constraint that may not at first appear to be a policy is the *corporate bonus plan.* If management is paid a bonus based on profitability, then it may attempt to build inventory levels, knowing that current period production expenses will be allocated to that inventory, effectively increasing profits. The existence of this policy can be discovered by making inquiries with the production scheduling staff, which will likely have experienced some unexplained pressure from management to increase production levels.

Yet another policy constraint is *overtime avoidance.* Plant managers are frequently judged on their ability to keep employee overtime levels to a minimum in order to reduce labor expenses. However, when the occurrence of overtime can keep the constrained resource operational, the resulting increased throughput should easily outweigh any overtime costs. This constraint can be spotted by investigating the reasons for downtime at the constrained resource.

A policy that causes considerable trouble for the constrained resource is the concept of attaining *production line balance.* Under this concept, the best production process is one where there is just barely a sufficient level of production capacity in all work centers to complete the work listed in the production schedule. This approach assumes that costs can be stripped out of the production process by deliberately limiting capacity levels in all areas. The problem with it is that any production shortfall in any work center will almost certainly limit the production of the constrained resource, and so will reduce throughput. This policy is readily apparent in most cases, because it takes a great deal of deliberate effort to achieve product line balance. A form of indirect evidence of line balancing is when constraints appear to crop up in many places, and will seem to move around the production floor even during a single day.

The constraint can sometimes be a shortage of raw materials. When this happens, the reason may be a policy that the company *will not pay for overnight delivery charges, or will only buy materials below a set maximum price.* Though these policies may reduce shipping charges or material costs, they will also starve operations of necessary materials, so that a reduction in material costs is offset by a much larger reduction in throughput. The existence of this policy can be discovered through discussions with the purchasing and production planning employees.

Policy constraints can even arise in the capital budgeting area, where *net present value* is the benchmark standard used to calculate the need for new equipment. However, this evaluation technique may result in the rejection of a proposed purchase from which incremental sprint capacity is to be gained, which in turn reduces the amount of potential downtime at the constraint. The proposal may clearly result in more throughput, but the traditional analysis model would not accept it. This policy can be found by investigating rejected capital budget proposals or by reviewing the project acceptance criteria in the capital budgeting procedure.

As mentioned in Chapter 1, perhaps the worst constraint is the general belief that a company *must run all of its resources at their maximum levels* in order to gain the highest level of efficiency and therefore (supposedly) the highest level of profit. This is not precisely a policy constraint, since it is not always formally enunciated, but is more of a "paradigm constraint," where everyone's underlying view of the production process is that all resources are to be run "flat out." In reality, only the constrained resource must be run at the highest level of efficiency, while many other resources should operate only when needed. This constraint is most easily spotted by checking work center efficiency reports for areas that are not constrained resources.

Another bad paradigm constraint is an *excessive focus on cost reduction.* When managers spend all of their time determining how to squeeze the last nickel out of their operations expenses, it is easy to lose sight of the resulting drop in production capacity that occurs as those expenses are gradually eliminated. Unrestricted cost reduction can eliminate large amounts of capacity, until a company has essentially cut so many expenses that it has run itself out of business. This type of policy is readily apparent when the bonus plan and management reports focus more on expenses than throughput.

Most of the policy constraints noted in this section share one bond—they are based on the concept of local optimization. Each one is designed to optimize a specific performance measurement, rather than the throughput of the entire system. For example, banning overtime will reduce labor costs, not paying delivery charges will cut freight costs, and long production runs will cut the average setup cost. However, in each case, they also reduce the total amount of throughput generated. Because of this common underlying problem, it is useful to analyze every production policy and determine if it is based on local optimization. If so, it is probably having a negative impact on throughput, or has the potential to do so.

Because it takes no investment or new expenses to overturn a policy constraint, there can be a massive payback involved in the adjustment or elimination of selected policies. However, this is rarely a simple task. Employees consider many production policies to be "set in stone," perhaps because of their training, but also simply due to habit. This makes it extremely difficult to convince employees that long-cherished policies are causing production problems. Unless thwarted, these policies can recur over time, as new employees take over job functions without proper indoctrination in throughput accounting concepts.

Given the number of examples shown in this section, it is evident that a production process may be rife with policy constraints. Accordingly, one should devote a considerable amount of time to the investigation of all policies that could impact throughput.

Having covered numerous aspects of the constrained resource, including its location, management, and mitigation, we will now move on to the use of buffers, which are a key tool for enhancing the productive efficiency of the constraint.

THE CONSTRAINT BUFFER

As described in Chapter 1, the buffer of inventory placed immediately in front of the constrained resource is critical to the throughput maximization of the constraint because the buffer protects the constraint from a work shutdown caused by a shortage of processed materials coming from upstream workstations. An inadequate buffer will result in periods when there are no materials to feed the constraint, yielding a throughput decline just as severe as if the constraint itself were mismanaged. These shortages can be caused by a wide array of production problems that are bound to occur to some degree, despite a company's best efforts to root out their causes. Though it may be possible to reduce the size of these production variations, there will *always* be variations—and the buffer is used to protect the constraint from them. If the level of production variation is high, then the protective buffer will be commensurately large, while smaller variations will call for the use of a much smaller buffer.

If a company has minimal excess capacity in its non-constraint areas, it will have an extremely difficult time recovering from a production shortfall, since it is only barely able to keep up with the demands of the constrained resource. This will likely result in a very long time to rebuild the inventory buffer if the buffer has been reduced to cover a production shortfall. Consequently, if there is a minimum amount of excess production capacity upstream from the constraint, management must choose between maintaining a large buffer or investing in more excess capacity. Since it is difficult to establish a large buffer in the first place (because there is so little excess capacity), the only real choice is to invest in extra capacity or tolerate stock-out conditions at the constraint.

This does not mean that a company should invest in inordinate amounts of excess capacity throughout its facility—far from it. Instead, managers can measure the amount of capacity that would have been needed to rebuild inventory buffers within a reasonable time period, and then only invest in that incremental amount of capacity. If the capacity problem relates to a work center that uses labor, rather than machine time, then the appropriate response is to engage in enough employee cross-training to ensure that staffing levels can be rapidly increased if a significant amount of extra inventory is needed.

An alternative to increasing the size of the inventory buffer is to intentionally replace it with so much upstream sprint capacity that the system can very rapidly replenish inventory shortages in front of the constrained resource. However, this is not normally a cost-effective solution, since capacity increases are usually much more expensive than incremental increases in inventory at the buffer. However, it can be a useful technique if used solely to address recovery from very large upstream variances that would otherwise call for the use of an inordinately large buffer.

For example, a common scenario is that a company suffers from an unexpected production shortage—perhaps one day of downtime caused by a power outage. Once service is restored, the company president realizes that this production shortfall will eliminate an entire day of throughput. There are a number of possible solutions from which the president may choose:

- *Do nothing.* Accept the possibility of a power outage and the associated loss of throughput. This is a reasonable alternative if there is a minimal history of outages, and no expectations of additional ones. The president essentially accepts the occurrence of a random event, and takes no risk mitigation steps.
- *Install a power generator.* This approach may work if there is a continual history of power problems, and especially if only a limited amount of electricity is needed to run a few key operations during the outage period.
- *Create an inventory buffer.* If there is a significant risk of additional outages and the cost of power generators is too high, then the president should consider building up an inventory buffer that matches the amount of the typical outage period.
- *Create additional sprint capacity.* This allows the company to quickly recover from the lost production time. The high cost of this alternative only makes it acceptable when the amount of throughput that would otherwise be lost is extremely high, and when there is an expectation of frequent outages.

Thus, the use of buffers always presents a broad range of solutions, and even a range of investments within each proposed solution. In the previous example, the president can invest in a broad range of solutions—power generators, or inventory levels, or sprint capacity.

The buffer itself contains an inventory subset called the expedite zone. When the amount of inventory in the buffer is sufficiently reduced so that reserves held in the expedite zone are being used, there is now a reasonable possibility that the constrained resource may run out of materials. This triggers a notification to the materials manager to expedite the production of those parts needed to increase the buffer sufficiently to restore the expedite zone to full size.

In some cases where proper buffer management can have a large impact on throughput, there may even be a "buffer manager" whose sole responsibility is the monitoring and replenishment of the buffer.

The buffer manager will note the reason for delays causing buffer penetrations, and work with the production manager to mitigate these delays in the future. The buffer manager may also engage in *dynamic buffering*. This is the careful management of buffers and upstream capacity levels to achieve the smallest possible investment in inventory and sprint capacity to ensure that throughput levels are maximized at a cost-effective level. If a company uses a materials requirements planning (MRP) system, the buffer manager can sometimes use this system to engage in sensitivity analysis to determine the best buffer size.

A hole in the buffer occurs when a planned upstream work center does not complete work by the scheduled date and time, resulting in the late arrival of materials in the buffer. Usually, only a small number of upstream work centers cause these buffer holes. These work centers can be easily spotted by using a buffer penetration chart such as the one described in Chapter 8, Throughput and Performance Measurement and Reporting Systems, and reproduced in Exhibit 2.1. The report shows when buffer penetrations occur, and identifies the originating workstation. The buffer manager uses this report to target problem areas requiring immediate resolution.

Buffer management is somewhat different when the work involves primarily labor, rather than machines. In this case, each work area normally has a planned period of time in which to complete its work before sending work-in-process (or an activity) on to the next group of employees for additional processing. The planned work period assigned to each employee usually includes a small buffer. This buffer tends to be heavily used by employees, who often wait until the last possible

Date	Arrival Time Required	Actual Arrival Time	Originating Work Station	Cause of Delay
Sept. 11	9/11, 2 P.M.	9/12, 3 P.M.	Paint shop	Paint nozzles clogged
Sept. 14	9/14, 9 A.M.	9/16, 4 P.M.	Electrolysis	Power outage
Sept. 19	9/19, 10 A.M.	9/19, 4 P.M.	Electrolysis	Electrodes corroded
Sept. 19	9/19, 4 P.M.	9/25, 10 A.M.	Paint shop	Paint nozzles clogged
Sept. 23	9/23, 1 P.M.	9/24, 9 A.M.	Paint shop	Ran out of paint

EXHIBIT 2.1   BUFFER MANAGEMENT REPORT

moment to finish their tasks. This approach obviously wastes the total amount of available buffer time, since employees are frequently able to complete tasks well before their assigned dates. Commonly, a few employees will exceed their allotted time periods because of actual production problems, resulting in the job as a whole exceeding its completion date.

An alternative approach to management of a labor-intensive process is to determine the total buffer time assigned to all steps in the process, and then place the buffer at the end of the entire work sequence. By doing this, employees will have much tighter timelines and so will be less likely to require additional time to complete their work. If they do have problems that require additional time, then these problems will gradually reduce the size of the buffer positioned at the end of the process. However, the total amount of the time buffer that is used is likely to be substantially less than if the same buffer had been split into a series of smaller buffers, so it is more likely that the targeted completion date will be met. Thus, the use of time buffers for a labor-centric process results in a different positioning of the buffer—at the end of the entire process, rather than in front of the constrained resource.

In summary, proper management of the buffer placed in front of the constrained resource is crucial to the attainment of high throughput levels. The key factor in buffer management is the determination of the proper buffer size, which is also addressed in a case study in Chapter 10, Throughput Case Studies.

THE ASSEMBLY AREA BUFFER

All of the buffer discussion thus far has centered on the buffer positioned before the constrained resource. This is the key buffer, but a buffer should also be used in one other area.

A buffer is needed in front of the final assembly area. This is used to guard against any production shortfalls of materials *not* involving the constrained resource. By filling the assembly buffer with materials that have not passed through the constraint, there will be no reason for parts processed *at* the constraint to wait in the assembly area. This ensures the fastest possible delivery times, and therefore a high rate of throughput.

The assembly buffer will never contain inventory produced by the constrained resource. This is because, by definition, there is not enough inventory being generated by the constraint to build up a buffer at all. If it had sufficient excess capacity to build a buffer, then the resource would not truly be the constraint.

The same buffering management rules apply to the assembly buffer that were described in the last section; mainly, the buffer size should be commensurate with the variability of the flow of production coming into it.

Ensuring that a final assembly buffer is properly maintained is crucial to the generation of throughput, since even the best upstream constraint management will not yield throughput results until final assembly has been completed.

PRODUCTION SCHEDULING

The final key element of constraint management in the factory is the rope, which is the timed release of raw materials into the production process to ensure that a job reaches the constrained resource when it is needed. The person driving this work is the production scheduler, who must ensure that all non-constraint resources are working on the right jobs, and in the right sequence and batch quantities to meet the constrained resource's schedule. This section shows how constraint management is used to clarify and simplify the role of the production scheduler, and in so doing, describes the rope mechanism.

The production scheduler must handle a variety of conflicting demands—from customers who want deliveries right now, cost accountants who demand long production runs in order to run equipment more efficiently, and managers who may want to produce extra inventory in order to shift overhead costs out of the current period. And on top of these demands, they must try to make a number of conflicting metrics look as good as possible, such as minimal overtime, maximum on-time deliveries, and reduced inventory levels. As the remainder of this section will attest, constraint management is a highly effective tool for resolving conflicting demands.

The first issue a scheduler must deal with is the order of priority for jobs. The overriding corporate goal is to maximize total throughput, but the scheduler must ensure that *all* orders accepted by the company are delivered to customers in a timely manner. Thus, the maximization of throughput is a fine goal, but that is handled at a strategic level by top management. The production scheduler has been given a specific set of orders to fulfill, and must find a way to do so—irrespective of the throughput associated with each one. Consequently, the amount of throughput associated with a job is not a valid criterion for its order of production priority.

Instead, the production scheduler must work with other scheduling criteria. First in importance is any job that would otherwise be delivered late to the customer. No company can stay in business for long if it persistently delivers late; customers will simply find more reliable suppliers in the future. Next in importance is inventory that can be reworked. There are two reasons for this enhanced level of priority. First, rework usually sits in the production area until fixed, and so interferes with the flow of production. Second, it is frequently associated with specific customer jobs, and so must be completed in order to meet required ship dates. The third level of scheduling priority is all other jobs on a first-in first-out (FIFO) basis. This third priority covers most production scheduling jobs, and merely states that a customer order will be handled in the order in which it was received. However, if a job is currently located directly in front of the constraint, the constraint can process it at once, and other higher-priority jobs are delayed, then that job should be handled in front of other FIFO-scheduled jobs in order to maximize resource usage. There will also be cases where special customers will receive priority treatment, but this modified FIFO rule works well in most situations. The fourth level of priority is any in-house inventory replenishment. Thus, production is scheduled in the following order:

1. Orders in danger of being delivered late
2. Rework
3. All other customer orders sequenced as of their receipt dates, subject to their physical location near the constrained resource
4. Inventory replenishment

Expediters may still be used in a constraint management scenario, but only for orders that would otherwise be delivered late. By requiring that all other orders follow the above priorities, a company will experience a relatively smooth flow of orders through its production area.

Production priorities are impossible to assign if the scheduler is basing her scheduling calculations on an unreasonable amount of available constraint time. For example, the absolute maximum number of minutes available at the constraint per week is 10,080 minutes (7 days × 24 hours × 60 minutes). However, this assumes that the resource is actually operational for that period of time, which is virtually never the case. There will be downtime for both preventive and unscheduled maintenance, as well as stoppages caused by raw material or work-in-process shortages, or staffing problems. There may be a number of other "Murphy's Law" issues that will further reduce the amount of available capacity, so the actual available amount of time is substantially lower than 10,080 minutes per week. Consequently, the production scheduler should only formulate a schedule based on the average number of constraint minutes available, based on a rolling average over the past few weeks or months.

A similar limiting factor in the determination of available constraint time is the consideration of how many batches will be run by the constrained resource, and in what size. An excessive number of small jobs and related setups will adversely impact the number of minutes available at the constraint. This issue is covered in the following section.

Another factor in the production scheduling task, besides the amount of available constraint time, is the amount of available labor. Labor costs are theoretically more fixed than variable, and so are irrelevant to the scheduling decision, on the assumption that there will be sufficient labor capacity to meet all reasonable production scheduling requirements. However, there are some types of processing that require specific types of skilled labor that may not be so readily available. If so, the production scheduler must also make use of a labor capacity planning model that multiplies the prospective production schedule by the types of labor required, as noted in the labor routing files, in order to compare the amount of required labor to available resources. This may result in rescheduling to match available labor resources.

The scheduler must also guard against excessive levels of production. This occurs when management insists on high levels of work center efficiency in *all* parts of the company. When this happens, there will be an increase in the level of work-in-process throughout the facility, since the overall flow of production is still limited by the pace of production at the constraint. Instead, proper scheduling should only address immediate production needs at the constraint, plus or minus any planned changes to inventory buffers.

Another scheduling issue is the timing of the release of raw materials into the production process. The production scheduler should never release materials too early nor in excessive quantities, because this merely clutters the work area with a large amount of inventory that is not yet needed, and which can confuse the production staff regarding which waiting work-in-process items should be processed next. Instead, raw materials should be released at the pace of the constraint, so that the materials arrive at the constraint buffer shortly before they are needed, and only in the amounts needed. The timing of materials release can be calculated as the time required to keep the constraint buffer full, plus the processing time required by all operations upstream of the constrained resource. This calculation is shown in one of the case studies in Chapter 10, Throughput Case Studies.

The avoidance of early raw materials release also applies if a job is missing engineering specifications, key materials, or tooling. If any of these elements are missing, there is no reason to launch a job into production, because it will merely clutter the production area until the missing components arrive.

There is also a strong production scheduling tendency to impose a large number of concurrent jobs on the production staff. When this happens, work centers keep shifting between multiple projects, with the result that their focus becomes diluted, and all jobs are delivered later than scheduled. A better approach is to reduce the number of jobs allowed into production to an optimum amount that can be discerned through trial and error. This reduced number sharpens the focus of the production staff, resulting in faster job completion.

This job release approach runs contrary to many scheduling systems, where customers want to hear that their orders are "in production," even if this only means that their order is languishing somewhere on the shop floor until such time as the manufacturing staff can get to it.

Finally, when work-in-process inventory *leaves* the constraint, there should be sufficient downstream production capacity to use labor routings to estimate the effort required to predict the final ship date. It is then possible to use this calculated ship date to work backwards and accurately determine the material release dates for other items that do not need to pass through the constraint operation. By doing so, all items required for final assembly, no matter what course they may follow through the production process, will arrive at the final assembly area with sufficient time to meet the shipment date.

In summary, the production scheduler must use a combination of scheduling priorities, realistic constraint capacity estimates, labor constraint planning, minimal non-constraint production, and restrictive material releases to ensure that throughput will be optimized. These are the basic tenets of the *rope* element of the drum-buffer-rope constraint management system.

In the next section, we will expand upon the use of batch sizing to maximize the number of available constraint minutes.

BATCH SIZES

Batch sizing is a key aspect of constraint management, because it impacts the rate at which inventory reaches the constrained resource, and therefore the amount of throughput to be realized. This section covers the impact of smaller batch sizes on overall throughput.

The inventory buffer situated in front of the constrained resource must be maintained at an adequate size, or else there is a heightened chance that the constraint will run out of materials, thereby reducing throughput. Though it is always possible to invest in a larger inventory buffer (if upstream capacity will allow it), an alternative scenario is apparent in Exhibit 2.2. In the exhibit, Case A reveals a buffer requiring a maximum stocking level of 100 units in order to ensure that buffer holes never reach the expedite zone. This stocking level is mandated by the use of large batch sizes, whereby the buffer is drawn down to low levels while large inventory batches are being produced upstream. Case B shows the impact of half-sized batches, where smaller inventory amounts arrive more frequently. Because of the more rapid replenishment, inventory levels drop less drastically, allowing for a smaller (and less expensive) inventory buffer as shown in Case C. Also, because of the system's increased ability to quickly send

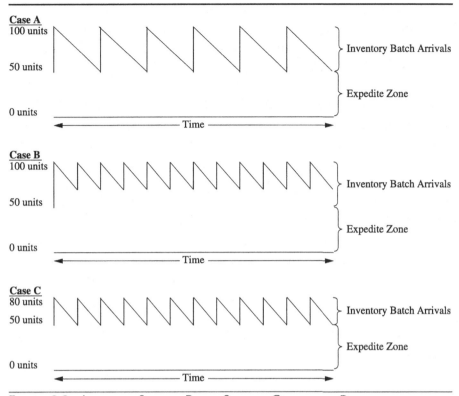

EXHIBIT 2.2   IMPACT OF SMALLER BATCH SIZES ON CONSTRAINT BUFFER

inventory replenishments to the buffer, it would also be possible to reduce the size of the expedite zone.

Though smaller batch sizes clearly have a favorable impact on the size of the inventory buffer, it would seem reasonable that the much larger number of setups would make this concept prohibitively expensive. However, we are talking about increasing the number of batches *upstream* from the constrained resource, not *at* the constraint. Because these upstream work centers have excess capacity, there is no cost associated with the extra setups—they are free. Consequently, the production scheduler could theoretically continue to schedule ever-smaller jobs in front of the constraint until such time as the extra setup burden requires the incremental addition of operating expenses. If a company has a large amount of excess capacity in these areas, it could therefore afford to schedule exceedingly small job sizes.

An entirely different scenario arises when batch sizing is applied to the constrained resource. In this case, the production scheduler must be much more careful in allocating the limited number of available production minutes toward job setups, since many setups for small jobs results in fewer minutes of available production time, and therefore a reduced level of throughput. Because of this issue, the scheduler has a tendency to plan for larger production runs at the constraint than in other work centers. The decision to authorize a longer production run than needed is based on the belief that any excess inventory will be rapidly sold off, so the scheduler must balance the savings from reduced setup time against the estimated time that extra production will be held in inventory prior to being sold.

One way to handle batch sizing at the constraint is to use bulk rate pricing management. For example, one could offer bulk-rate discounts to customers, thereby convincing them to place a smaller number of large orders. This pricing decision makes sense to the company, because it offsets the reduced throughput on the lower price point with its added capacity from avoiding an excessive number of setups.

In summary, small batch sizing is a no-cost option when jobs are passing through non-constraint work centers, but will be the subject of intense analysis when it involves the constrained resource. In the next two sections, we will examine another aspect of the batch sizing issue, which is the time required to set up a machine for each batch.

MACHINE SETUPS—SALES PERSPECTIVE

The sales staff does not like small customer orders, because they have been told by the cost accounting staff that the cost of equipment setups must be spread over such a small number of units that the cost of production will eliminate any profits from the prospective sale. This is a misconception, because nearly all production work centers have so much excess capacity available that setups are essentially free. Only if a lengthy setup is required at the constrained resource will the company experience a reduction in throughput, since other products could have been created during the setup. Thus, machine setups should not play a roll in the acceptance of a small customer order, unless the setup occurs at the constraint.

MACHINE SETUPS—REDUCTION EFFORTS

Equipment setups are an important element of the production process, for setups can be lengthy, and can interfere with the level of throughput achieved. This section addresses where setup reduction efforts should be centered.

There is an entire science dedicated to the reduction of equipment setup times, involving video-taping the process, analyzing each portion of the setup, and finding a variety of ways to shrink the setup interval. Many companies triumphantly implement this process throughout their facilities, and have achieved remarkable setup reductions. However, there is one problem with this setup methodology—it only results in improved throughput if the setup reduction occurs at the constrained resource. If implemented on any other work center, a company will achieve the ability to set up jobs very quickly, but since there is already excess capacity, it does not achieve any additional throughput. Thus, the expense of working through the setup reduction effort will achieve no return on investment unless it is done on the constraint.

Companies that have achieved really excellent setup reductions can make a case that only through ongoing setup reduction practices can they achieve high setup reduction results. This line of reasoning leads to a mandate to work on setup reductions throughout the facility, sometimes well away from the constraint. This is not an entirely bad approach to setup reduction, for in addition to the additional experience obtained, it also gives a company more capacity throughout its facility, which means that it has better sprint capacity to recover from downtime situations. Nonetheless, the greatest setup reduction effort should always be centered on the constrained resource, since this results in the greatest improvement in throughput.

In summary, setup reduction is exceptionally useful at the constrained resource, since it results in more available minutes of production, which can be used to either generate more throughput or accept larger numbers of smaller jobs. Setup reduction efforts elsewhere in the company are good for practice and can yield increased sprint capacity, but have no direct impact on throughput.

SUMMARY

Constraint management in the factory centers on the identification and proper management of the drum, which is the constrained resource. As shown in this chapter, there are many ways to locate the constraint, as well as to improve its performance. Constraints can also be policies, the modification of which can improve throughput to a considerable extent. However, policies are ingrained in most organizations, and so require considerable effort to root out.

Running a close second in importance to constraint management is buffer management. The buffer shields the constrained resource from upstream production fluctuations. The proper sizing and ongoing management of the buffer is a major priority of the materials management function, since an excessively large buffer is a waste of working capital, while an insufficiently small one can cause material shortages that reduce throughput.

Finally, the production scheduler ensures that materials are released into the production process at the appropriate time to ensure that the constraint is fed with an adequate supply of materials. We addressed the impact of batch sizing and setup reduction efforts on the scheduling process, and how they can be used to maximize throughput.

In the following chapters, we turn to an examination of the impact of constraint management on the accounting function, including how it compares to other cost accounting systems, how it can be used in a variety of financial analysis and capital budgeting scenarios, and how it can be included in control and performance measurement systems.

3

THROUGHPUT AND TRADITIONAL COST ACCOUNTING CONCEPTS

The preceding chapter explained in some detail how constraint management works in the factory. Now we turn our attention to applying the constraint management concepts to the accounting department. In this chapter, we will compare throughput accounting to traditional cost accounting concepts, which address different areas of emphasis and reporting including system reporting instead of product- based reporting, throughput being more important than cost management, the elimination of most types of variance reporting, and why overhead allocation causes incorrect decisions. We will also compare throughput accounting to two other popular systems of cost accounting: activity-based costing and direct costing. By the end of this chapter, you should see that throughput accounting represents a major departure from traditional cost accounting concepts.

THE EMPHASIS ON COST VERSUS THROUGHPUT

In a traditional cost accounting environment, the accountant is trained to focus on product costs, usually in extraordinary detail, rather than on the ability of the company to generate profits. Conversely, throughput accounting is least concerned with costs and most concerned with using the existing system (and the costs built into it) to generate the largest possible amount of profit. Which concept is right?

Under the traditional cost accounting approach, if the accountant is solely reporting on the cost of operations, then it is reasonable for management's attention to be skewed in the direction of cost management, since this is the only information they see. However, nearly all costs fall into the Operating Expenses category of costs, and the primary purpose of that cost category is to support the ability of the company to produce throughput. Thus, an excessive degree of attention to cost reduction will eventually impact a company's ability to produce throughput, so that profits may decline even faster than any cost reductions that have been achieved.

This problem is especially difficult to perceive when the accountant identifies an excessive level of capacity in a non-constraint area, and proposes that the company save money by eliminating some portion of the excess capacity. What the accountant misses is how important that excess capacity may be. The total capacity at each work center should be divided into three parts. The first is *productive capacity,* which is that portion of the total work center capacity needed to process currently scheduled production. The second part is *protective capacity,* which is that additional portion of capacity that must be held in reserve to ensure that a sufficient quantity of parts can be manufactured to adequately feed the bottleneck operation. Any remaining capacity is called *idle capacity.* Only idle capacity can be eliminated from a work center.

If the capacity to be eliminated is protective capacity and not idle capacity, then the constrained resource will not have any inventory on which to work, and must shut down until its inventory inflow can be replenished. Thus, the reduction in capacity in order to cut costs may seem like a reasonable decision in the short term, until such time as a sufficiently large manufacturing problem results in a throughput drop precisely because of the missing capacity.

Throughput accounting takes the opposite approach to financial analysis, focusing instead on improving the utilization of the constrained resource in order to maximize profits through increases in throughput. It is designed to answer three questions regarding management decisions, which are:

1. What is the decision's impact on throughput (top priority)?
2. What is the decision's impact on investment (second priority)?
3. What is the decision's impact on operating expenses (last priority)?

The strong emphasis is on improving the first of these items, which is throughput. The reason operating expense reduction is given such low priority is that, as just noted, a large part of operating expenses are needed to support the system's capacity to create throughput.

In short, both systems focus on improvements to net profitability, but throughput accounting does so primarily by enhancing throughput, while traditional cost accounting focuses more on improvements to net profitability by reducing costs. Though both approaches are trying to achieve the same goal, throughput accounting relies more on top-line growth, which can potentially be infinitely expandable, while traditional cost accounting tries to cut costs from a finite pool of expenses, thereby limiting the potential amount of profit growth. Furthermore, cost reduction must be exercised with great care in order to avoid capacity cutbacks.

THE EMPHASIS ON PRODUCT COST VERSUS SYSTEM PROFITABILITY

A traditional cost accounting system requires the accountant to spend a great deal of time calculating the gross margin of each product, which includes a large proportion of allocated costs. Throughput accounting has no interest in the fully burdened cost of a product, focusing instead on enhancing the performance of the entire system.

A major result of this change in philosophy is the utilization level of work centers from which production is not currently needed. A traditional costing system would hold that it should continue to operate as much as possible with long production runs, on the grounds that the average cost per unit must be kept low by spreading the cost of the work center over the largest possible number of units. Throughput accounting would require the work center's operations to be stopped on the grounds that any additional output would simply result in a greater investment in inventory that the company does not need, as well as additional operating expenses to store the excess inventory. Furthermore, work stations operating upstream from the constrained resource should have relatively short production runs, which gives them the ability to quickly switch to the production of some other parts that may be needed in the near future at the constraint.

Furthermore, a throughput accountant is so concerned with the operation of the entire system that her primary reporting topic is the ability of the organization to exactly meet the scheduled production for the constrained resource, as well as for all other workstations. Thus, she will delve into the reasons why these schedules are not met—missing materials, improper manning, machine downtime, and so on. None of these activities are a common pursuit of the traditional accountant, who is only concerned with product costs.

Finally, allocating cost to products at all is considered nonsensical in a throughput environment, because most costs do not vary with production. Even the cost of direct labor rarely varies directly with the quantity of production, since managers prefer not to send employees home as soon as production stops. Only in those rare cases where employees are paid based on piece work should the cost of direct labor be charged to individual products. Logically, operating expenses should not be allocated because they represent the cost of running the entire system of production, and cannot be partitioned into small blocks of cost that can be assigned to a single product.

In short, the traditional accounting focus on product costs tends to result in excessive quantities of manufactured inventory. Throughput accounting focuses on the operation of the entire production system, resulting in much less inventory, lower work center utilization levels, and higher throughput.

VARIATIONS IN THE TREATMENT OF LOW-MARGIN PRODUCTS

There is a substantial difference in the manner in which low-margin products are treated under the traditional and throughput accounting systems. A traditional approach dictates that a great many overhead costs be assigned to each product (as described in the previous section). By doing so, product margins will be reduced considerably. In some cases, margins will likely become negative. Managers will then eliminate these products, under the false assumption that they are not earning the company a profit, and they would be better off without them. What actually happens is that no overhead costs are eliminated along with the canceled products. Instead, the same pool of overhead costs must now be spread over a smaller pool of remaining products, which increases the allocated cost per product, and makes the remaining products appear to be even *less* profitable. This can lead to a continuous series of product eliminations that leaves a company in a much less profitable situation than when it started eliminating its low-margin products.

For example, Acorn Company has three products, whose margins are shown in the following table. The company has $100,000 of overhead costs, which it allocates based on the number of units sold. Acorn sells a combined total of 15,000 units of all three of its products, so each one receives an overhead charge of $6.66 ($100,000 overhead expense/15,000 units).

	Product Alpha	Product Beta	Product Charlie	Totals
Units sold	1,500	3,500	10,000	15,000
Price each	$ 8.00	$12.00	$ 15.00	—
Variable cost each	3.00	5.00	6.00	—
Overhead allocation	6.66	6.66	6.66	—
Gross margin each	$ (1.66)	$ 0.34	$ 2.34	—
Gross margin total	$(2,490)	$1,190	$23,400	$22,100

Based on this analysis, Acorn elects to stop selling Product Alpha, which has a fully burdened loss of $2,490. The company does not lose any overhead expenses as a result of this product elimination, so the same $100,000 must now be allocated among products Beta and Charlie, resulting in an increased overhead charge per unit of $7.41 ($100,000 overhead expense/13,500 units). The results appear in the following table:

	Product Beta	Product Charlie	Totals
Units sold	3,500	10,000	13,500
Price each	$ 12.00	$ 15.00	—
Variable cost each	5.00	6.00	—
Overhead allocation	7.41	7.41	—
Gross margin each	$ (0.41)	$ 1.59	—
Gross margin total	$(1,435)	$15,900	$14,465

Now the Product Beta margin has become negative, with a fully burdened loss of $1,435. Acorn now stops selling Product Beta. Overhead expenses do not decline as a result of this product cancellation, so now the entire cost is allocated to Product Charlie, at a rate of $10.00 per unit ($100,000 overhead expense/10,000 units). The result is shown in the following table:

	Product Charlie
Units sold	10,000
Price each	$ 15.00
Variable cost each	6.00
Overhead allocation	10.00
Gross margin each	$ (1.00)
Gross margin total	$(10,000)

Based on the new cost allocation, Acorn cancels Product Charlie as well, and now finds itself out of business! Thus we have gone from a profitable company to a bankrupt one, just because a fixed pool of overhead costs is being allocated to individual products.

Under throughput accounting, a product is *only* eliminated if its price is lower than its totally variable costs. Since these totally variable costs usually include only direct materials, there will be very few circumstances where the product price will be low enough to warrant product elimination. Instead, all products are kept if they generate any positive throughput at all, since this will contribute to the overall throughput being generated by the production system, and will allow the company to pay for its operating expenses.

By using throughput accounting to retain allegedly low-margin products, a company will tend to have broader diversity in its product offerings. The assumption is that the company can continue to handle the extra labor required to keep track of these more diverse products, which can include a larger number of component parts, warranty claims, product designs, and so on. A case can be made in favor of product elimination only in situations where a specific amount of clearly defined operating expenses can be eliminated along with a product.

Throughput accounting uses the same concepts noted in this section to avoid the allocation of corporate overhead costs to individual operating divisions. Such an allocation merely masks the throughput of each division, and would run the risk of incorrectly selling off a division because it cannot cover its corporate overhead allocation, even tough it generates positive throughput. Also, allocation assumes that there is some relationship between the performance of the division and the corporate overhead costs, such that an increase in division throughput would trigger an increase in overhead costs (or vice versa), which is a false assumption.

In summary, a focus on throughput instead of allocated costs will result in greater profitability, few product cancellations, and a broader set of product offerings. The same philosophy should be applied at the corporate level, where the allocation of corporate expenses to operating divisions will only mask the ability of those divisions to generate throughput.

THE EMPHASIS ON BURDENED VERSUS THROUGHPUT PRICING

Traditional cost accounting methodology holds that pricing should include fully absorbed costs plus an acceptable profit margin. The reason for this thinking is that all costs must be covered for an adequate level of pricing, or else there will be no profit once all product and operating costs are subtracted from the total of all prices paid by customers. The sales and marketing staff chafes under this approach, since it is sometimes confronted with offers from customers to buy large quantities of product at reduced prices—but the accountants will not approve the lower prices, even if the proposed price points exceed the variable cost of the products.

However, throughput theory holds that *any* price point that exceeds the totally variable cost of a product should be considered. Proposed price points and unit volumes for incremental sales can then be included in a mix of current production activity to determine what the change will do to total throughput and the constrained resource. If the result improves throughput and there is a way to handle the increased production volume, then the price point is approved. Consequently, throughput accounting gives the sales staff a much greater degree of flexibility in setting pricing. The sales staff does not need to wade through a complex absorption costing formula for each product that it needs to price. Instead, all it needs is the proposed price, the totally variable cost of the product under consideration, and a discussion with the production scheduling staff to see if the proposed job can be scheduled into the constrained resource without hurting other scheduled production.

For example, the Tasmanian Chutney Company (TCC) has received a request for a special garlic-flavored chutney, at a price of $1.50 per jar. TCC applies a standard overhead charge of $0.40 to each jar of chutney produced. When this overhead cost is added to the $1.25 variable cost of producing a jar of garlic-flavored chutney, TCC's cost accountant calculates that there will be a loss of $0.15 per jar, and so rejects the proposed order. However, a throughput analysis of the pricing proposal is included in the following table of TCC's various products, which shows a positive throughput of $0.25 per jar, because the overhead allocation is ignored for pricing purposes. Thus, TCC should accept the offer if there is sufficient production capacity to handle the order.

Chutney Flavor	Price/Jar	Variable Cost	Overhead	Net Profit	Throughput
Apple	$2.80	$1.80	$0.40	$0.60	$1.00
Peach	2.55	1.65	0.40	0.50	0.90
Banana	2.40	1.60	0.40	0.40	0.80
Garlic	1.50	1.25	0.40	(0.15)	0.25

There are several objections to the exclusion of overhead costs from the pricing formula. First, it may result in extremely low price points that will not allow a company to cover all of its expenses, which results in a loss. Over the long term, this is an accurate assessment. However, in the short term, if a company has excess production capacity available and can use it to sell additional product that generates throughput, then it should do so in order to increase profits. If its production capacity is already maximized, then proposed sales having lower throughput levels than items already being manufactured should be rejected.

Second, traditional accounting holds that a small proposed order that requires a lengthy machine setup should have the cost of that setup assigned to the product; if the additional cost results in a loss on the proposed transaction, then the sale should be rejected. However, throughput accounting does not include the cost of setups in the totally variable cost of the product, since it assumes that the company's existing production capacity can absorb the cost of the incremental setup without incurring any additional cost. Under this logic, if there is excess production capacity, then setups are free. This approach tends to result in a company offering a much richer mix of order sizes and products to its customers, which can yield a greater market share. However, this concept must be used with caution, for at some point the ability of the company to continually set up small production jobs will maximize its capacity, at which point there will be an incremental cost to adding more production jobs.

The third issue arises not from traditional cost accounting, but from federal government pricing rules. If a company enters into a contract to offer products or services to the federal government at a certain predetermined price, a key provision of the contract will be that the government will automatically receive the lowest price offered by the company to any of its customers. Consequently, when reviewing new pricing proposals, the sales staff should be mindful of how a new price point will impact any existing sales to and throughput arising from transactions with the federal government.

Thus far, the discussion of pricing has focused on the minimum acceptable price. It is also important to note that there is no reason to tie a product's upper price limit to its cost. Instead, the upper price point should be whatever price the market will accept. Though this is not a precept of throughput accounting or traditional cost accounting, there is a greater tendency in traditional cost accounting to establish a price based on the underlying product cost plus a standard margin percentage.

In short, throughput accounting results in more pricing flexibility for the sales staff, since a product's totally variable cost represents the lowest possible price point, rather than a fully burdened cost.

VARIATIONS IN SCRAP REPORTING

There is a significant difference between traditional and throughput accounting in the reporting of scrap. Under traditional cost accounting, the cost of any scrapped item will be its fully absorbed cost. For example, the following table shows that a product passing through a series of work centers will accumulate the cost of each work center, and will have a progressively higher scrap cost if it is scrapped later in the production process.

Work Center	Work Center Cost Added	Work Center Cumulative Cost	+	Product Variable Cost	=	Total Scrap Cost
No. 1	$2.05	$ 2.05		$8.25		$10.30
No. 2	0.35	2.40		8.25		10.65
No. 3	1.15	3.55		8.25		11.80
No. 4	4.80	8.35		8.25		16.60
No. 5	1.80	10.15		8.25		18.40

Throughput accounting takes a different approach, where the location of the constrained resource dictates the cost of the scrap. If scrap occurs prior to the constrained resource, then the cost of the scrap is strictly the variable cost of the work-in-process, which is usually only its material cost. No additional cost is assigned based on the number of work centers involved in processing the scrapped item because these upstream workstations have excess capacity, and so can easily process replacement inventory for free. The basic concept for this type of scrap is that a work center's production capability is free as long as it has excess capacity.

Under throughput accounting, the cost assignment scenario changes radically if scrap occurs either at the constrained resource or anywhere downstream from it. If scrap occurs in these areas, it must be replaced with another part that will use up additional time at the constrained resource. Thus, the cost of scrap occurring either at or following the constrained resource is the lost throughput that would have been realized if the item had not been scrapped. The calculation of post-constraint scrap is itemized in Chapter 8, Throughput and Performance Measurement and Reporting Systems. In brief, it is to compile the constraint hours spent to produce all scrap occurring at or after the constraint, and then multiply this by the average throughput per hour generated by the constraint.

The preceding scrap example is presented again below, but now we assume that the constrained resource is Work Center 3. In the example, we assume that the average throughput per hour generated by the constrained resource is $2,000, and that one unit of a scrapped item requires three minutes of operating time by the constrained resource, which translated to an opportunity cost of $100 ($2,000 × 3/60).

Work Center	Throughput Opportunity Cost	+	Product Variable Cost	=	Total Scrap Cost
No. 1	$ 0.00		$8.25		$ 8.25
No. 2	0.00		8.25		8.25
No. 3	100.00		0		100.00
No. 4	100.00		0		100.00
No. 5	100.00		0		100.00

The treatment of scrap reporting has a major impact on where a company should install quality assurance workstations or invest in quality improvements. Under the traditional costing system, the gradual accumulation of costs in scrap tends to result in more quality assurance work towards the end of the production process, where scrap costs per unit are higher. However, this emphasis is much greater in a throughput accounting environment, where the cost of scrap anywhere after the constrained resource is astronomically higher than before it. Thus, a throughput-driven system would always put a quality assurance station directly in front of the constrained resource in order to remove low-quality work-in-process before it can waste the time of the constrained resource. Also, quality improvement investments at or downstream from the constrained resource are an excellent idea, since they prevent the loss of constraint time.

For example, the Candy Stripe Company, maker of two-tone toothpaste, is evaluating a proposal to reduce the scrap rejection rate of its product. The company is currently throwing out 1,000 tubes of tooth-paste per hour, all downstream of the constrained resource. Its constrained resource is the packaging machine, which uses a multi-nozzle dispenser to fill different colors of toothpaste into the toothpaste tube. The machine produces 5,000 tubes of toothpaste per hour, which is $2,500 of throughput per hour. The proposal is intended to eliminate downstream bursting of the tubes due to overfilling, and requires an investment of $250,000 in a replacement multi-nozzle dispenser that more precisely fills each tube. The dispenser will require replacement once a year.

All scrap is downstream from the constraint, so the average hourly throughput rate of $2,500 is the appropriate cost to apply to the scrap. The scrap rate is 20 percent of hourly production, so the scrap cost is 20 percent of the average hourly throughput rate, or $500 per hour. If the company invests in the new multi-nozzle dispenser, it will require 500 hours of throughput to repay the investment ($250,000 investment/$500 per hour of throughput savings). Since the company runs on an eight-hour day, this means that the investment will be recouped in just over two months, leaving nearly ten more months in which to generate additional throughput from the investment. Thus, the investment proposal should be accepted.

In summary, throughput accounting presents a major change in the costing of scrap. Rather than assigning an accumulated overhead cost based on how far inventory has come in the production process before being scrapped, throughput accounting holds that the scrap cost varies massively based on the simple criterion of whether it occurs before or after the constrained resource.

VARIATIONS IN VARIANCE ANALYSIS

Variance analysis is a major task for the accountant schooled in traditional cost accounting logic. At the end of each reporting period, the accountant is expected to generate variances for the price of all materials, labor, and overhead from budgeted price levels; as well as efficiency variances for the use of materials, labor, and variable overhead; and finish with a volume variance calculation related to the application of fixed overhead. All of this analysis is designed

Variance Type	Material	Labor	Variable Overhead	Fixed Overhead
Price Variance	Yes	Yes	Yes	Yes
Efficiency Variance	Yes	Yes	Yes	No
Volume Variance	No	No	No	Yes

EXHIBIT 3.1 SUMMARY-LEVEL REVIEW OF VARIANCE COMPONENTS

to give management a detailed view of how closely the company adheres to its budgeted levels of input prices, production volumes, and work center efficiencies. The various types of variances are shown in Exhibit 3.1.

There are several problems with this kind of variance analysis. First, it is based on a budget that may have little basis in reality, and that may contain many negotiated numbers designed to enhance the reported performance of the more politically astute managers. For example, if the purchasing manager inserts into the budget an expected materials price that is too high, then the reported materials price variance will be favorable, possibly resulting in this manager receiving an undeserved bonus.

Second, variance analysis reports on some variances over which management has little control, rendering them useless. For example, the overhead volume variance measures the impact on profitability of variations in the amount of applied overhead, based on the difference between the actual and budgeted quantities of an activity; thus, profit is altered based on the application of an overhead pool over which management has little control over the short term.

Third, the use of efficiency variances create an incentive for managers to operate their resources at very high levels of utilization, whether than utilization is needed or not. The result is invariably an excessive level of inventory, since some workstations are producing more inventory than can be readily handled by downstream workstations. Thus, it is impossible to achieve both the high local efficiencies engendered by variance analysis and the low inventory levels required for proper production management.

Finally, variance analysis has no focus on the constrained resource. Instead, it focuses on the efficiency and cost of operation of each individual part of the production system, rather than the ability of the entire system to generate a profit. As a result, a company may find that it achieves excellent efficiency and price variances by having long production runs and buying in large quantities, only to find that its net profit has vanished due to an excessively high investment in inventory and far too much work-in-process clogging the production area.

A system focused on constraint management will likely show very poor results under a variance reporting system, because it appears to operate inefficiently on a local level. For example, when a workstation upstream from the constrained resource runs out of work, a manager operating under throughput accounting assumptions will shut it down in order to avoid the creation of an excessive level of work-in-process inventory. However, this will cause a negative labor efficiency variance, since the work center's staff is not actively producing anything. For this reason, most work centers other than the constrained resource should have a low labor efficiency level.

Throughput accounting does use variance analysis, but not the ones used by a traditional system. Instead, its primary focus is on tracking variations in the size of the inventory buffer placed before the constrained resource, to ensure that the constraint is never halted due to an inventory shortage. This analysis is conducted with a Buffer Management Report and Buffer Hole Percentage Trend Report, which are shown in Chapter 8, Throughput and Performance Measurement and Reporting Systems.

THE TREATMENT OF DIRECT LABOR

The treatment of direct labor varies considerably between traditional cost accounting and throughput accounting. Under traditional accounting, direct labor is charged to each product as a variable cost. It should rarely be charged to a product as though it were a variable expense, because it is not. Direct labor does not vary in proportion to the volume of units produced, unless there are very substantial changes in the unit volume of production. Instead, direct labor usually constitutes a limited pool of skilled laborers who work the same number of hours each day, regardless of the volume of work to be completed. Managers cannot afford to have these employees go home when there is no additional production work to be done, since there is a significant risk that they will go elsewhere to find work that provides a more consistent level of pay. Instead, managers keep them on site, either doing other work or continuing to produce more inventory than is needed. For these reasons, "direct" labor is certainly not direct. Once again, only in piece work situations where the production staff is paid for each incremental unit of production is there a reason to charge the cost of labor to a product.

A second improper use of direct labor under traditional cost accounting is to designate direct labor as the basis upon which overhead expenses will be allocated to inventory. This is an unsound practice for two reasons. First, direct labor does not vary directly with the level of production, as just explained, so it forms a poor basis upon which to allocate inventory. Second, overhead costs are not allocated under throughput accounting, since these costs have nothing to do with the incremental cost to create a product—they only represent the cost of maintaining a certain level of production capacity for the system as a whole.

Throughput accounting takes a much more simplified view of direct labor, which is that, since it is essentially a fixed cost, it is included in operating expenses, and is treated as a cost of maintaining a certain level of throughput capacity. Its cost is not charged to products.

INVENTORY VALUATION

Traditional cost accounting and throughput accounting treat inventory valuation in fundamentally different ways. Traditional costing mandates that some portion of direct labor and overhead expenses be assigned to all inventory. By doing so, these expenses are removed from the income statement and stored on the balance sheet until such time as the inventory is consumed, when the expenses are recognized on the income statement. There are two problem with this approach. First, the underlying assumption that operating expenses are related to the volume of inventory produced is incorrect; instead, operating expenses represent the ability of the system to create throughput during a specific period of time. Whether the system operates at zero percent or 100 percent utilization during that period has minimal impact on the amount of operating expense incurred, so the entire expense should be written off during the current period. Second, because traditional costing allows inventory to absorb costs, managers have a tendency to create more inventory than needed in order to improve their reported level of profitability, which has the adverse side effects of increasing both inventory storage costs and the company's investment in working capital.

Throughput accounting uses the minimalist approach of only assigning to the value of inventory the cost of the materials consumed in its production, on the grounds that these are the only totally variable costs involved. This method results in the complete elimination of any incentive for managers to produce excessive quantities of inventory because they can no longer improve their financial results by storing operating expenses in inventory.

ACTIVITY-BASED COSTING VERSUS THROUGHPUT ACCOUNTING

One of the more popular accounting methodologies is activity-based costing (ABC), which (as the name implies) allocates overhead costs based on a cost object's use of various activities. The ABC process starts with the allocation of costs from the general ledger to several cost pools. Next, we select activity drivers that are closely associated with the costs in each of the cost pools, and then derive a cost per unit of activity. Finally, we accumulate the number of units of each activity used by each cost object (such as a product or customer) and multiply this number by the cost per activity driver. The result is a complete allocation of all overhead costs to the cost objects in a logical manner. For more details on this complicated process, see the author's book, *Cost Accounting* (John Wiley & Sons, 2001).

There are several problems with ABC. First, it requires a considerable amount of time to set up and operate on an ongoing basis, because of the massive data gathering required. Second, ABC will highlight various cost objects that appear to use an inordinate amount of resources; managers will be more likely to focus their attention on the reduction of resource usage by these cost objects, which may be scattered throughout the facility. The problem is that ABC does not recognize the existence of a resource constraint, instead putting the spotlight on a multitude of areas whose improvement may not yield any increase in throughput, though they may reduce operating expenses. Third, ABC allocates costs to products, which not only can shift current period expenses into inventory, but also incorrectly assumes that a certain amount of operating expense is directly tied to the production of each incremental unit of production.

However, ABC works well in labor-intensive production environments. In these cases, labor resources are more flexible, allowing production constraints to be overcome with relative rapidity. An ABC system will penalize those jobs that consume excess amounts of production labor, resulting in an emphasis on products that use parsimonious amounts of the more labor-intensive production activities.

Throughput accounting ignores the resource consumption issues that ABC highlights, focusing instead on throughput issues at the constrained resource. This is the fundamental difference between the two systems—ABC targets operating expense reduction, which is considered the least important variable in a throughput accounting system, trailing throughput maximization and investment reduction.

Throughput accounting is also much easier than ABC to calculate, as it completely avoids any attempt to create cost pools, identify cost drivers, or allocate costs based on those drivers. Instead, no attempt is made to allocate operating expenses at all, on the assumption that operating expenses are period costs, and so should not be allocated.

Throughput accounting tends to yield better results in machine-intensive production areas. Where machine usage is prevalent, machines pace the flow of operations and are the primary cost, leaving little room for opportunities to alter costs over the short term. With costs relatively fixed, throughput accounting is a perfect tool for focusing attention on throughput enhancement.

In short, ABC is a complicated system to create and maintain, and tends to focus management attention primarily on operating expense reduction. Throughput accounting considers operating expense reduction to be a lesser concern, and so makes no attempt to allocate operating expenses to any type of cost object.

DIRECT COSTING VERSUS THROUGHPUT ACCOUNTING

Direct costing is sometimes considered to be the same costing concept as throughput accounting, because direct costing focuses on the incremental profit to be gained by subtracting variable costs from a product's price. This concept is also used by throughput accounting, though many direct costing practitioners still consider direct labor to be a variable cost, and so subtract it from a product's price to arrive at a gross margin.

There are two key differences between the two concepts. First, throughput accounting also factors the impact of incremental changes in investment and operating expenses into its decision models, whereas direct costing is solely concerned with gross margin analysis. Second, the primary purpose of throughput accounting is to monitor the system's ability to generate throughput, whereas direct costing is concerned with localized decisions involving incremental changes in gross margin.

In short, throughput accounting is a more comprehensive system than direct costing, integrating both constraint and throughput analysis into the basic margin analysis used by direct costing.

SUMMARY

This chapter has shown that traditional cost accounting suffers from several problems. First, it cannot produce usable information because it assumes that all of a company's resources are equally important. This incorrect focus results in local optimization to enhance variances, when instead the performance of the entire system should be considered. Local optimization also results in excessive inventory levels because work centers are being operated longer than necessary. Second, traditional accounting focuses tightly on the cost of individual products, including allocated overhead costs. This results in smaller product margins, and even negative margins that lead to the decision to cancel some products. Third, it requires that product pricing be sufficient to cover an overhead allocation charge, thereby possibly resulting in the loss of some sales.

Throughput accounting concentrates all attention on the proper servicing of the constrained resource in order to maximize system throughput. It accepts local inefficiencies as long as this results in maximum throughput, low inventory levels, and minimized operating expenses (in that order). Variance analysis is largely ignored, with the exception

Costing System	Capacity Utilization	Capital Budgeting	Cost Reduction	External Financial Reporting	Internal Management Reporting	Inventory Valuation	Outsourcing Decisions	Pricing	Process Improvement	Product Design	Product Mix	Product Profitability	Scrap Costing
Activity-Based Costing			X	X	X	X	X	X	X			X	X
Direct Costing		X			X		X	X	X			X	
Job Costing			X	X		X		X				X	
Joint and Byproduct Costing				X		X						X	
LIFO, FIFO, Average Costing				X		X							
Process Costing				X		X		X				X	
Standard Costing								X				X	X
Target Costing			X		X			X		X		X	
Throughput Costing	X		X		X		X	X	X		X		X

EXHIBIT 3.2 USES OF ACCOUNTING SYSTEMS

of variances resulting in buffer penetration. Product pricing has an established floor, which is a product's totally variable costs; this can result in additional throughput, depending the company's capacity to produce.

Finally, comparisons were made to the activity-based costing and direct costing systems, showing how throughput accounting compares favorably to them. For a more comprehensive view of where throughput accounting fits into the various accounting methodologies, it is included in the costing systems matrix in Exhibit 3.2. This exhibit shows the various uses for nine different accounting systems, ranging from activity-based costing through throughput accounting. A perusal of the matrix shows that throughput accounting is useful for most types of accounting, with the notable exception of financial reporting. That topic will be covered in Chapter 6, Throughput and Generally Accepted Accounting Principles.

4

THROUGHPUT AND FINANCIAL ANALYSIS SCENARIOS

Throughput accounting is a superb methodology for arriving at the correct solution to a number of financial analysis scenarios. As such, this chapter is critical to an understanding of how constraint management can be used in multiple aspects of a business. This chapter contains many financial analysis scenarios, with each one containing an example of how throughput accounting can be used to arrive at the correct decision. For easy reference, the analysis scenarios listed in this chapter are as follows:

1. The low price, high volume decision
2. The low price for export market decision
3. The outsourced production decision
4. The increased downstream capacity decision
5. The increased upstream product processing decision
6. The increased sprint capacity decision
7. The additional quality workstation decision
8. The increased constraint staffing decision
9. The new product addition decision
10. The product cancellation decision
11. The altered product priority decision
12. The raw material constraint decision
13. The constraint in the marketplace decision
14. The plant closing decision

In addition, be sure to review the Underlying Concepts of the Throughput Analysis Model section near the end of this chapter. It gives the analyst useful information about the assumptions used to construct the model, which may prevent it from being used incorrectly.

THE BASIC THROUGHPUT ANALYSIS MODEL

The primary focus of throughput accounting is on how to force as much throughput dollars as possible through the capacity constraint. It does this by first determining the throughput dollars per minute of every production job scheduled to run through the capacity constraint, and rearranging the order of production priority so that the products with the highest throughput dollars per minute are completed first. The system is based on the supposition that only a certain amount of production can be squeezed through a bottleneck operation, so the production that yields the highest margin must come first in order of production scheduling priority, to ensure that profits are maximized. The concept is most easily demonstrated in the example shown in Exhibit 4.1.

In the example, we have four types of products that a company can sell. Each requires some machining time on the company's capacity constraint, which is the circuit board manufacturing process (CBMP). The first item is a 19-inch color television, which requires four minutes

Product Name	Throughput $/Minute of Constraint	Required Constraint Usage (minutes)	Units of Scheduled Production	Constraint Utilization (minutes)	Throughput per Product
1. 19″ Color television	$8.11	4	500/500	2,000	$ 16,220
2. 32″ LCD television	7.50	6	350/350	2,100	15,750
3. 50″ High definition TV	6.21	10	150/150	1,500	9,315
4. 42″ Plasma television	5.00	12	180/400	2,160	10,800
		Total planned constraint time		7,760	—
		Maximum constraint time		8,000	—
			Throughput total		$ 52,085
			Operating expense total		47,900
			Profit		$ 4,185
			Profit percentage		8.0%
			Investment		$320,000
			Return on investment*		15.7%

*Annualized

EXHIBIT 4.1   THE THROUGHPUT MODEL

of the CBMP's time. The television sells for $100.00, and has associated direct materials of $67.56, which gives it a throughput of $32.44 (the price and direct materials cost are not shown in the exhibit, only inferred). We then divide the throughput of $32.44 by the four minutes of processing time per unit on the capacity constraint to arrive at the throughput dollars per minute of $8.11 that is shown in the second column of the exhibit. We then calculate the throughput per minute for the other three products, and sort them in high-low order, based on which ones contribute the most throughput per minute. This leaves the 19-inch color television at the top of the list. Next, we multiply the scheduled production for each item by the time required to move it through the constrained resource. We do this for all four products, and verify that the total planned time required for the constraint operation is equal to or less than the actual time available at the constraint, as shown in the "Total planned constraint time" row. In the exhibit, the maximum available constraint time is listed in bold as 8,000 minutes, which is the approximate usage level for an eight-hour day in a 21-day month of business days, assuming 80 percent efficiency. This number will vary dramatically, depending on the number of shifts used, scrap levels, and the efficiency of operation of the constrained resource.

A key concept is that the maximum number of units of the highest throughput-per-minute item (in this case, the 19-inch color television) are to be sold, as well as the maximum volume for each product listed below it. Only the production volume of the product listed at the bottom of the table (in this case, the 42-inch plasma television) will be reduced in order to meet the limitations of the constrained resource. The amount of planned production as well as the amount of potential sales are shown in the "Units of Scheduled Production" column of the throughput model. For example, "500/500" is shown in this column for the 19-inch color television, which means that there are 500 units of potential sales for this product, and the company plans to produce all 500 units. Only for the last product in the table, the 42-inch plasma television, do the units of production not match the potential sales (180 units are being produced instead of the 400 units of potential sales). By doing so, a company can maximize throughput.

Then, by multiplying the throughput per minute by the number of minutes for each product, and then multiplying the result by the total number of units produced, we arrive at the total throughput for each product, as shown in the final column, as well as for the entire production process for the one-month period, which is $52,085. However, we are not done yet. We must still subtract from the total throughput the sum of all operating expenses for the facility, which is $47,900 in the exhibit. After they are subtracted from the total throughput, we find that we have achieved a profit of 8.0 percent and a return on investment (annualized, since the results of the model are only for a one-month period) of 15.7 percent.

This is the basic throughput financial analysis model, incorporating all the key throughput analysis elements of throughput dollars, operating expenses, and return on investment. It will be used as the foundation for a number of financial analysis scenarios in this chapter. When reviewing a proposal with this model, one must review the impact of the decision on the incremental change in net profit caused by a change in throughput minus operating expenses, divided by the change in investment. If there is an incremental improvement in the model, then the proposed decision should be accepted. The model makes it easy to determine the exact amount of system improvement (or degradation) occurring by incrementally changing one element of the production system.

THE LOW PRICE, HIGH VOLUME DECISION

What happens when a customer indicates that a very large order is about to be issued—but only if the company grants a significant price reduction? The typical analysis is for the cost accountants to determine the fully burdened cost of the product in question, compare it to the low requested price, and then reject the proposal out of hand because they state that the company cannot cover its overhead costs at such a low price point. Conversely, the sales manager will ram through approval of the proposal, on the grounds that "we will make up the loss with higher volume." Which is right? Based on their logic, neither one, because they are not considering the net impact of this proposal on the total system throughput. Perhaps the following example will clarify the situation.

The sales manager of the electronics company in our previous example runs into the corporate headquarters, flush from a meeting with the company's largest account, Electro-Geek Stores (EGS). He has just agreed to a deal that drops the price of the 32-inch LCD television by 20 percent, but which guarantees a doubling in the quantity of EGS orders for this product for the upcoming year. The sales manager points out that the company may have to hold off on a few of the smaller-volume production runs of other products, but no problem—the company is bound to earn more money on the extra volume. To test this assumption, the cost accountant pulls up the throughput model on his computer, shifts the LCD TV to the top of the priority list, adjusts the throughput to reflect the lower price, and obtains the results shown in Exhibit 4.2.

To be brief, the sales manager just skewered the company. By dropping the price of the LCD television by 20 percent, much of the product's throughput was eliminated, while so much of the capacity constraint was used up that there was little room for the production of any other products that might generate enough added throughput to save the company. Specifically, because of its low level of throughput dollars per minute, the planned production of the 42-inch plasma television had to be dropped from 180 units to just 25, nearly eliminating the throughput of this product.

This example clearly shows that one must carefully consider the impact on the capacity constraint when debating whether to accept a high-volume sales deal. This is a particularly dangerous area in

Product Name	Throughput $/Minute of Constraint	Required Constraint Usage (minutes)	Units of Scheduled Production	Constraint Utilization (minutes)	Throughput per Product
1. 32" LCD television	$4.36	6	700/700	4,200	$ 18,312
2. 19" Color television	8.11	4	500/500	2,000	16,220
3. 50" High definition TV	6.21	10	150/150	1,500	9,315
4. 42" Plasma television	5.00	12	25/400	300	1,500
		Total planned constraint time		8,000	—
		Maximum constraint time		8,000	—
			Throughput total		$ 45,347
			Operating expense total		47,900
			Profit		$ (2,553)
			Profit percentage		(5.6%)
			Investment		$320,000
			Return on investment*		(9.6%)

*Annualized

EXHIBIT 4.2 THE LOW PRICE, HIGH VOLUME DECISION

which to ignore throughput accounting, for the acceptance of a really large-volume deal can demand all of the time of the capacity constraint, eliminating any chance for the company to manufacture other products, and thereby eliminating any chance of offering a wide product mix to the general marketplace.

THE LOW PRICE FOR EXPORT MARKET DECISION

A problem confronting many companies is whether or not to sell on the international market. In many cases, this requires the use of an unusually low price point in order to meet the competitive pressures of the marketplace. The decision to go this route may appear correct in the short term, since the company can generate additional throughput with the incremental sales. However, if entering the export market also requires a long-term contract with a local distributor, then the company may be locked into the lower export price for some time. This could hurt the company if local demand for its other products increases, and it cannot fulfill the local demand.

For example, the company is considering the possibility of selling its 32-inch LCD television in the burgeoning Slovenian market, for which a local distributor has placed an initial order of 360 units. To do so, the company must accept a lower price point that translates into a throughput per unit of $31.50. Since the product requires six minutes of constraint time, this translates into throughput per minute of $5.25. This level of throughput per minute places the exported LCD television fourth in priority in the throughput model, as shown in Exhibit 4.3. Because the LCD television now has two different prices and therefore two different levels of throughput, it is listed twice in the throughput model, once at each throughput level.

The model reveals that, because the throughput is higher for the export model than the lowest-throughput product listed in the table (the 42-inch plasma television), the company will earn a larger profit by producing more of the export model and less of the plasma television.

THE OUTSOURCED PRODUCTION DECISION

Another common decision to consider is whether to outsource production. The usual analysis will focus on the reduced margin that the

Product Name	Throughput $/Minute of Constraint	Required Constraint Usage (minutes)	Units of Scheduled Production	Constraint Utilization (minutes)	Throughput per Product
1. 19″ Color television	$8.11	4	500/500	2,000	$ 16,220
2. 32″ LCD television	7.50	6	350/350	2,100	15,750
3. 50″ High definition TV	6.21	10	150/150	1,500	9,315
4. 32″ LCD TV (export)	5.25	6	360/360	2,160	11,340
5. 42″ Plasma television	5.00	12	20/400	240	1,200
		Total planned constraint time		8,000	—
		Maximum constraint time		8,000	—
			Throughput total		$ 53,825
			Operating expense total		47,900
			Profit		$ 5,925
			Profit percentage		11.0%
			Investment		$320,000
			Return on investment*		22.2%

*Annualized

EXHIBIT 4.3   THE LOW PRICE FOR EXPORT MARKET DECISION

company will earn, since the supplier will likely charge a higher price than the company can achieve if it keeps the work in house. However, the correct view of the situation is whether the company can earn more throughput on a combination of the outsourced production and the additional new production that will now be available through the constrained resource.

One of the company's key suppliers has offered to take over the entire production of the 50-inch high definition television, package it in the company's boxes, and drop ship the completed goods directly to the company's customers. The catch is that the company's throughput per unit will decrease from its current $62.10 to $30.00. The cost accounting staff would likely reject this deal on the grounds that profits would be reduced. To see if this is a good deal, we turn once again to the throughput model, which is reproduced in Exhibit 4.4. In this exhibit, we have removed the number from the "Units of Scheduled Production" column for the high definition television, since it can now be produced without the use of the capacity constraint. However, we are still able to put a cumulative throughput dollar figure into the final column for this product, since there is some margin to be made by outsourcing it through the supplier. By removing the high definition television's usage of the capacity constraint, we are now able to produce more of the next product in line, which is the plasma

Product Name	Throughput $/Minute of Constraint	Required Constraint Usage (minutes)	Units of Scheduled Production	Constraint Utilization (minutes)	Throughput per Product
1. 19″ Color television	$8.11	4	500/500	2,000	$ 16,220
2. 32″ LCD television	7.50	6	350/350	2,100	15,750
3. 50″ High definition TV	3.00	10	150/150	N/A	4,500
4. 42″ Plasma television	5.00	12	325/400	3,900	19,500
		Total planned constraint time		8,000	—
		Maximum constraint time		8,000	—
			Throughput total		$ 55,970
			Operating expense total		47,900
			Profit		$ 8,070
			Profit percentage		14.4%
			Investment		$320,000
			Return on investment*		30.3%

*Annualized

EXHIBIT 4.4   THE OUTSOURCED PRODUCTION DECISION

television set. This additional production allows the company to increase the amount of throughput dollars, thereby creating $3,885 more profits than was the case before the outsourcing deal.

Once again, the traditional cost accounting approach would have stated that profits would be lowered by accepting an outsourcing deal that clearly cost more than the product's internal cost. However, by using this deal to release some capacity at the bottleneck, the company is able to earn more money on the production of other products.

THE INCREASED DOWNSTREAM CAPACITY DECISION

An excellent role for the accountant is in the analysis of capital budgeting proposals, since a close examination of them using the throughput analysis model will reveal that many of them are not necessary. In particular, it is rarely necessary to invest in additional capacity downstream from the constrained resource, since it does nothing to increase a company's throughput.

For example, the industrial engineering manager has been reviewing a number of workstations in the production area, and finds that they can speed up the production capacity of the circuit board insertion machine, which is the next workstation in line *after* the constrained resource. They can double the speed of the insertion machine if the company is willing to invest an extra $50,000. To see if this is a good

Product Name	Throughput $/Minute of Constraint	Required Constraint Usage (minutes)	Units of Scheduled Production	Constraint Utilization (minutes)	Throughput per Product
1. 19″ Color television	$8.11	4	500/500	2,000	$ 16,220
2. 32″ LCD television	7.50	6	350/350	2,100	15,750
3. 50″ High definition TV	6.21	10	150/150	1,500	9,315
4. 42″ Plasma television	5.00	12	180/400	2,160	10,800
		Total planned constraint time		7,760	—
		Maximum constraint time		8,000	—
			Throughput total		$ 52,085
			Operating expense total		47,900
			Profit		$ 4,185
			Profit percentage		8.0%
			Investment		$370,000
			Return on investment*		13.6%

*Annualized

EXHIBIT 4.5 THE INCREASED DOWNSTREAM CAPACITY DECISION

idea, we once again look at the throughput model. In this instance, the only number we change is the investment amount, since actual throughput will not increase. The results are shown in Exhibit 4.5.

By making the extra investment, the only change in the company's situation is that its return on investment has dropped by more than 2 percent. The reason is that any investment used to improve any operation besides the capacity constraint is a waste of money. The only thing that a company achieves by making such an investment is that it has improved the efficiency of an operation that will still be controlled by the speed of the capacity constraint. In reality, the situation is even worse, for any newly upgraded downstream operation will now have greater efficiency, and can therefore produce in even greater quantities—all of which will turn into work-in-process that will pile up somewhere further downstream in the production process. Thus, an investment in a non-constrained operation will probably worsen the overall financial results of the company, because its overall investment and its investment in inventory will increase.

THE INCREASED UPSTREAM PRODUCT PROCESSING DECISION

It is sometimes possible to increase the capacity of the constrained resource by shifting more of the work tasks being handled at that resource to a work center located upstream from it. This shifting of work carries with it the danger of increasing the workload so substantially on the upstream work center that it becomes the constrained resource. Nonetheless, when scheduled judiciously, this approach can increase throughput.

For example, the company's industrial engineering staff has determined that it can increase the speed of the capacity constraint from 8,000 available minutes per month to 8,800 minutes, but only if additional processing work is completed by the machining operation just before the constraint operation, which will cost $4,000 in operating expenses and reduce the available capacity of the preceding operation by 28 percent. As Exhibit 4.6 shows, this is quite a good idea, for we can now process more units of the 42-inch plasma television that we were previously unable to schedule, creating an additional profit of over $5,000; the added usage of a non-constrained operation makes no difference, since it is simply improving the rate of throughput at the constrained resource.

A traditional cost accounting analysis might have rejected this proposal, because the cost of the additional machining time on the preceding workstation would have been added to the cost of any products running through it, which would have increased their fully burdened price, thereby making their margins supposedly too low to be profitable.

Product Name	Throughput $/Minute of Constraint	Required Constraint Usage (minutes)	Units of Scheduled Production	Constraint Utilization (minutes)	Throughput per Product
1. 19″ Color television	$8.11	4	500/500	2,000	$ 16,220
2. 32″ LCD television	7.50	6	350/350	2,100	15,750
3. 50″ High definition TV	6.21	10	150/150	1,500	9,315
4. 42″ Plasma television	5.00	12	266/400	3,192	15,960
		Total planned constraint time		8,792	—
		Maximum constraint time		8,800	—
			Throughput total		$ 57,245
			Operating expense total		51,900
			Profit		$ 5,345
			Profit percentage		9.3%
			Investment		$320,000
			Return on investment*		20.0%

*Annualized

EXHIBIT 4.6   THE INCREASED UPSTREAM PRODUCT PROCESSING DECISION

THE INCREASED SPRINT CAPACITY DECISION

Production shortfalls can occur at many locations in the production process, and can be considered inevitable, since it is impossible to guard against the multitude of possible system failures. If these production shortfalls occur upstream from the constrained resource, then there is a strong likelihood that the flow of materials into the constraint will be impeded, which will reduce throughput and profits. To guard against this problem, it is useful to incorporate an excessive level of production capacity into the production process. This "sprint capacity" gives the company the opportunity to produce at well above normal production rates in order to catch up from failure episodes. The proper way to analyze the need for more sprint capacity is to determine the history of throughput shortfalls caused by the lack of sprint capacity, and compare the lost throughput to the cost of adding sprint capacity, to see if the investment is cost-effective.

For example, one of the company's standard management reports is the buffer hole trend report shown in Exhibit 4.7. The report shows an upper and lower boundary line, which represent tolerable boundaries for the percentage of all jobs where production problems caused the buffer to be penetrated. The small circles represent the daily percentage of jobs causing buffer penetration, while the line running approximately through the center of the boundary limits is a multi-day moving average

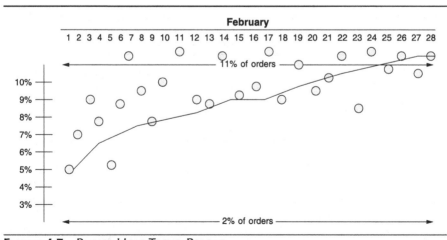

EXHIBIT 4.7 BUFFER HOLE TREND REPORT

of the percentage of expedited orders experienced. The report reveals that the buffer is being penetrated with increasing regularity, and that roughly one-third of all days now result in penetration levels exceeding the tolerable limit.

The management team investigates the reason for these buffer penetrations and determines that problems in the integrated circuit assembly operation, located upstream from the constrained operation, are not only causing the problem but are also likely to continue for the near future. The buffer penetrations have limited the available constraint time per month from the usual 8,000 minutes to just 6,500 minutes, with the adverse results shown in Exhibit 4.8.

Clearly, the loss of throughput is resulting in significant losses, and must be remedied by the addition of sufficient sprint capacity to restore profitability by bringing the maximum available constraint time per month back to 8,000 minutes. To do so, the company must invest $80,000 in additional integrated circuit assembly equipment, as well as one person to operate it, who will cost $3,500 per month. The results are shown in Exhibit 4.9.

This analysis shows that investing in additional sprint capacity will restore some degree of profitability to the company. However, the investment also yields only a minimal level of profitability, so the company's managers must continue to try resolving the production problems that have required this investment.

Product Name	Throughput $/Minute of Constraint	Required Constraint Usage (minutes)	Units of Scheduled Production	Constraint Utilization (minutes)	Throughput per Product
1. 19″ Color television	$8.11	4	500/500	2,000	$ 16,220
2. 32″ LCD television	7.50	6	350/350	2,100	15,750
3. 50″ High definition TV	6.21	10	150/150	1,500	9,315
4. 42″ Plasma television	5.00	12	75/400	900	4,500
		Total planned constraint time		6,500	—
		Maximum constraint time		6,500	—
			Throughput total		$ 45,785
			Operating expense total		47,900
			Profit		$ (2,115)
			Profit percentage		(4.6)%
			Investment		$320,000
			Return on investment*		(7.9)%

*Annualized

EXHIBIT 4.8   IMPACT OF BUFFER PENETRATIONS ON THROUGHPUT MODEL

Product Name	Throughput $/Minute of Constraint	Required Constraint Usage (minutes)	Units of Scheduled Production	Constraint Utilization (minutes)	Throughput per Product
1. 19" Color television	$8.11	4	500/500	2,000	$ 16,220
2. 32" LCD television	7.50	6	350/350	2,100	15,750
3. 50" High definition TV	6.21	10	150/150	1,500	9,315
4. 42" Plasma television	5.00	12	180/400	2,160	10,800
		Total planned constraint time		**7,760**	—
		Maximum constraint time		**8,000**	—
			Throughput total		$ 52,085
			Operating expense total		51,400
			Profit		$ 685
			Profit percentage		1.3%
			Investment		$400,000
			Return on investment*		2.1%

*Annualized

EXHIBIT 4.9 RESULT OF ADDING UPSTREAM SPRINT CAPACITY

THE ADDITIONAL QUALITY WORKSTATION DECISION

The placement of a quality review workstation in the production area can have a major impact on profitability. If placed just in front of the constrained resource, it keeps low quality items from using up valuable processing time at the constraint. If these work-in-process items were to pass through the constrained resource and then be thrown out as scrap, then the capacity of the constraint used to produce them would have essentially been wasted. In this case, the correct analysis is to weigh the cost of the additional quality review staff and equipment against the throughput saved by not running all detected scrap through the constrained resource.

For example, one quality review person is to be hired for a new testing station at a rate of $30 per hour, or $5,040 per month ($30/hour × 8 hours/day × 21 business days), and will need $10,000 of new testing equipment. Based on a history of scrap detected downstream of the constrained resource, this should reduce scrap levels by 12 percent before it reaches the constraint, which thereby effectively increases the constrained resource's capacity from 8,000 minutes to 8,960 minutes per month. An example of the quality workstation decision is shown in Exhibit 4.10.

The exhibit shows that removing bad product prior to the constrained resource created a sufficient level of additional throughput to easily

Product Name	Throughput $/Minute of Constraint	Required Constraint Usage (minutes)	Units of Scheduled Production	Constraint Utilization (minutes)	Throughput per Product
1. 19" Color television	$8.11	4	500/500	2,000	$ 16,220
2. 32" LCD television	7.50	6	350/350	2,100	15,750
3. 50" High definition TV	6.21	10	150/150	1,500	9,315
4. 42" Plasma television	5.00	12	280/400	3,360	16,800
		Total planned constraint time		8,960	—
		Maximum constraint time		8,960	—
			Throughput total		$ 58,085
			Operating expense total		52,940
			Profit		$ 5,145
			Profit percentage		8.9%
			Investment		$330,000
			Return on investment*		18.7%

*Annualized

EXHIBIT 4.10 THE ADDITIONAL QUALITY WORKSTATION DECISION, UPSTREAM

offset the cost of the quality review person, as well as the incremental equipment investment.

However, what if the quality review station were to be shifted a few yards to the other side of the constrained resource? This would mean that no constraint time would be saved, while the company would still be investing in the additional staff person and equipment. The result is shown in Exhibit 4.11, where there is no change in throughput, but an increase in expenses and invested capital that changes the company's profit to a loss.

Product Name	Throughput $/Minute of Constraint	Required Constraint Usage (minutes)	Units of Scheduled Production	Constraint Utilization (minutes)	Throughput per Product
1. 19" Color television	$8.11	4	500/500	2,000	$ 16,220
2. 32" LCD television	7.50	6	350/350	2,100	15,750
3. 50" High definition TV	6.21	10	150/150	1,500	9,315
4. 42" Plasma television	5.00	12	180/400	2,160	10,800
		Total planned constraint time		7,760	—
		Maximum constraint time		8,000	—
			Throughput total		$ 52,085
			Operating expense total		52,940
			Profit		$ (855)
			Profit percentage		(1.6)%
			Investment		$330,000
			Return on investment*		(3.1)%

*Annualized

EXHIBIT 4.11 THE ADDITIONAL QUALITY WORKSTATION DECISION, DOWNSTREAM

Consequently, merely moving the quality workstation to one side or the other of the constrained resource can have a significant impact on corporate profitability, either up or down.

THE INCREASED CONSTRAINT STAFFING DECISION

When a company starts using constraint management as its guiding principle in managing throughput, an early area of decision making will be how to increase the output of the constrained resource. An obvious first step is to add staff to it, with the intent of achieving faster equipment setup time, less equipment downtime, more operational efficiency per machine, and so on. As long as the incremental increase in throughput exceeds the cost of each staff person added to the constraint, this should be a logical step to take. However, traditional cost accounting analysis will likely find that the additional labor assigned to the constrained resource will not be needed at all times, would therefore have a low level of efficiency, and would reject the proposal.

For example, the company realizes that it can vastly reduce job setup time by adding an employee to the constrained resource, thereby increasing the maximum constraint time from 8,000 minutes per month to 8,800 minutes. Due to scheduling issues, the employee must be assigned to the constrained resource for an entire eight-hour day, even though she is only needed for a total of one hour per day. Her cost is $25 per hour, or $4,200 per month ($25/hour × 8 hours × 21 business days). The result of this change is shown in Exhibit 4.12.

The exhibit reveals that the company can use the extra capacity to build more units of the 42-inch plasma television, resulting in $5,160 of additional throughput that, even when offset against the $4,200 additional labor cost (which has been added to the operating expense line item), still results in an incremental profit improvement of $960. The main problem is that the employee will be working on the constrained resource for only one hour out of eight, which is a 12.5 percent utilization percentage that will certainly draw the attention of the cost accounting staff. Consequently, low incremental labor efficiency on the constrained resource can make sense if the resulting incremental throughput exceeds the cost of the labor.

Product Name	Throughput $/Minute of Constraint	Required Constraint Usage (minutes)	Units of Scheduled Production	Constraint Utilization (minutes)	Throughput per Product
1. 19" Color television	$8.11	4	500/500	2,000	$ 16,220
2. 32" LCD television	7.50	6	350/350	2,100	15,750
3. 50" High definition TV	6.21	10	150/150	1,500	9,315
4. 42" Plasma television	5.00	12	266/400	3,192	15,960
		Total planned constraint time		8,792	—
		Maximum constraint time		8,800	—
			Throughput total		$ 57,245
			Operating expense total		52,100
			Profit		$ 5,145
			Profit percentage		9.0%
			Investment		$320,000
			Return on investment*		19.3%

*Annualized

EXHIBIT 4.12   THE INCREASED CONSTRAINT STAFFING DECISION

THE NEW PRODUCT ADDITION DECISION

When adding a new product that requires use of the constrained resource, management may be startled to find that profits actually decline as a result of the introduction, because the new product eliminated an old product that yielded more throughput per minute. The traditional cost accounting system will not spot this problem, because it focuses on the profitability of a product, rather than the amount of the constrained resource needed to produce it.

For example, the company's engineers have designed a new, lower-cost 32-inch LCD television to replace the existing model. The two products are compared in Exhibit 4.13.

The traditional cost accountant would review this comparative exhibit and conclude that the new model is clearly better, since it

	32" LCD Television (New)	32" LCD Television (Old)
Price	$ 400	$ 400
Totally variable costs	$ 340	$ 355
Throughput	$ 60	$ 45
Overhead allocation	$ 35	$ 35
Profit	$ 25	$ 10
Required constraint usage	10 minutes	6 minutes
Throughput per minute of constraint	$6.00	$7.50

EXHIBIT 4.13   COMPARISON OF OLD AND NEW TELEVISION MODELS

costs less to build, resulting in a profit $15 greater than the old model. However, the new model achieves less throughput per minute, because its larger throughput is being spread over a substantial increase in the required amount of time on the constrained resource. By replacing the old model with the new model, we arrive at the results shown in Exhibit 4.14.

The model shows that profits have declined by $570, because the new model has used up so much constraint time that the company is no longer able to produce as many of the 42-inch plasma televisions. Furthermore, the throughput per minute on the new product has declined so much that it is now ranked as the third most profitable product, instead of occupying the new two position, as was the case for its predecessor product.

Let us now modify the analysis so that the company's product engineers have spent their time reducing the required amount of constraint time for the 32-inch LCD television, rather than in reducing its cost. In fact, let us assume that they *increase* the product's cost by $5 while *reducing* the amount of required constraint time from six minutes to five minutes, which increases its throughput per minute to $8.00. The result is shown in Exhibit 4.15, where the company's total throughput has increased, because more time is now available at the constrained resource for additional production of the plasma television. However,

Product Name	Throughput $/Minute of Constraint	Required Constraint Usage (minutes)	Units of Scheduled Production	Constraint Utilization (minutes)	Throughput per Product
1. 19" Color television	$8.11	4	500/500	2,000	$ 16,220
2. 50" High definition TV	6.21	10	150/150	1,500	9,315
3. 32" LCD television (new)	6.00	10	350/350	3,500	21,000
4. 42" Plasma television	5.00	12	83/400	996	4,980
		Total planned constraint time		7,996	—
		Maximum constraint time		8,000	—
			Throughput total		$ 51,515
			Operating expense total		47,900
			Profit		$ 3,615
			Profit percentage		8.0%
			Investment		$320,000
			Return on investment*		13.6%

*Annualized

EXHIBIT 4.14 THE NEW PRODUCT ADDITION DECISION (LOWER COST)

Product Name	Throughput $/Minute of Constraint	Required Constraint Usage (minutes)	Units of Scheduled Production	Constraint Utilization (minutes)	Throughput per Product
1. 19" Color television	$8.11	4	500/500	2,000	$ 16,220
2. 32" LCD television (new)	8.00	5	350/350	1,750	14,000
3. 50" High definition TV	6.21	10	150/150	1,500	9,315
4. 42" Plasma television	5.00	12	229/400	2,748	13,740
		Total planned constraint time		7,998	—
		Maximum constraint time		8,000	—
			Throughput total		$ 53,275
			Operating expense total		47,900
			Profit		$ 5,375
			Profit percentage		10.1%
			Investment		$320,000
			Return on investment*		20.2%

*Annualized

EXHIBIT 4.15 THE NEW PRODUCT ADDITION DECISION (HIGHER THROUGHPUT/MINUTE)

this new product introduction would almost certainly have been canceled by the cost accountants, because the cost per unit would have increased.

THE PRODUCT CANCELLATION DECISION

Products are usually canceled because their fully burdened costs exceed their prices. However, the cancellation decision is being driven by a false assumption, which is that the overhead costs being charged to the product will disappear once the product is canceled. In reality, the overhead costs will remain, and will now be allocated to other products. Only when a product's totally variable cost exceeds its price should it be canceled. Also, a company may elect to stop producing a product that has less throughput than other products that use all of the constrained resource's available capacity—however, even then it may be possible to outsource its production, if the resulting outsourced cost still results in some positive throughput.

For example, the company has just completed a lengthy activity-based costing analysis that has altered its allocation of overhead costs to products. It is now apparent that much more overhead than was previously thought to be the case must be charged to the high definition television. This results in a clear loss for the product. Accordingly, the

Product Name	Throughput $/Minute of Constraint	Required Constraint Usage (minutes)	Units of Scheduled Production	Constraint Utilization (minutes)	Throughput per Product
1. 19″ Color television	$8.11	4	500/500	2,000	$ 16,220
2. 32″ LCD television	7.50	6	350/350	2,100	15,750
3. 50″ High definition TV	6.21	10	—	—	—
4. 42″ Plasma television	5.00	12	325/400	3,900	19,500
		Total planned constraint time		7,760	—
		Maximum constraint time		8,000	—
			Throughput total		$ 51,470
			Operating expense total		47,900
			Profit		$ 3,570
			Profit percentage		6.9%
			Investment		$320,000
			Return on investment*		13.3%

*Annualized

EXHIBIT 4.16 THE THROUGHPUT MODEL

cost accounting manager writes a memo to the management team, outlining his reasons for requesting that the company immediately stop manufacturing this product. To see what effect this will have on company profits, we return to the throughput model, as noted in Exhibit 4.16, and eliminate the scheduled production for the high definition television. Since we have already maximized all output of the top two products, this means that we add more units of the 42-inch plasma television to use up the extra constraint time that is now available.

The result is a profit reduction of $615, because the additional plasma televisions that took the place of the high definition television have a lower level of throughput per minute of constraint time.

THE ALTERED PRODUCT PRIORITY DECISION

The basic throughput model is designed around the incremental through generated by each product in the production schedule. What if the cost accounting staff decides to use the traditional cost accounting measure of gross margin instead of throughput to determine the order of priority in the throughput model? This means that allocated overhead costs will be included in the determination of how a product is prioritized in the model.

Product Description	Throughput	Overhead Allocation	Gross Margin	Required Constraint Usage (minutes)	Throughput $/Minute of Constraint	Gross Margin $/Minute of Constraint
19" Color television	$32.44	$23.32	$ 9.12	4	$8.11	$2.28
32" LCD television	45.00	22.20	22.80	6	7.50	3.80
50" High definition TV	62.10	33.00	29.10	10	6.21	2.91
42" Plasma television	60.00	12.00	48.00	12	5.00	4.00

EXHIBIT 4.17   FULLY ABSORBED PRODUCT COSTS

For example, the company's cost accounting manager does a thorough activity-based costing analysis of all four products and determines that, after all overhead costs are properly allocated, the 42-inch plasma television actually has the highest gross margin, and the 19-inch television has the least. The relative positions of the other two products do not change. The cost accounting manager's summary of the newly revised product costs appears in Exhibit 4.17.

According to the cost accounting scenario, we should actually be producing as many 42-inch plasma television sets as possible. To test this theory, we will move the plasma television to the top of the list and produce all 400 units that are on order (rather than just the 180 units for which capacity has traditionally been available), while dropping the 19-inch television to the bottom of the list, and only producing as many units as will still be available after all other production has been completed. All other variables will stay the same. This analysis is shown in Exhibit 4.18.

According to this analysis, there has been a net *reduction* in throughput from $52,085 to $46,581! How can this be possible if we just used a detailed cost allocation process to match overhead costs to products? The trouble is that overhead costs do not actually vary with each incremental unit produced, and so they cannot be charged against an individual product. By doing so, there is a risk of disguising the true throughput of each product, with the adverse results shown in Exhibit 4.18.

THE RAW MATERIAL CONSTRAINT DECISION

What if a company experiences a shortage in the amount of available raw materials? This problem occurs when suppliers have too many

Product Name	Throughput $/Minute of Constraint	Required Constraint Usage (minutes)	Units of Scheduled Production	Constraint Utilization (minutes)	Throughput per Product
1. 42″ Plasma television	5.00	12	400/400	4,800	$ 24,000
2. 32″ LCD television	7.50	6	350/350	2,100	15,750
3. 50″ High definition TV	6.21	10	110/150	1,100	6,831
4. 19″ Color television	8.11	4	0/500	—	—
		Total planned constraint time		8,000	—
		Maximum constraint time		8,000	—
			Throughput total		$ 46,581
			Operating expense total		47,900
			Profit		$ (1,319)
			Profit percentage		(2.8)%
			Investment		$320,000
			Return on investment*		(4.9)%

*Annualized

EXHIBIT 4.18   THE ALTERED PRODUCT PRIORITY DECISION

orders in comparison to their available capacity, and place their customers on an allocation basis. It can also happen when problems occur in the supplier-to-company distribution system, such as bad weather, a train derailment, shipwreck, and so on. When any of these problems arise, the constraint is no longer located at an in-house work center, but rather in the raw material. When this happens, we must alter the throughput model so that the second column is changed from the throughput per minute of constraint time to throughput per raw material unit.

For example, the company has been placed on allocation for the random access memory (RAM) chips that it uses in all of its television products. This change is shown in Exhibit 4.19, where the production priorities are now substantially different, because each product uses different quantities of the RAM chips in comparison to the amounts of throughput they generate. Also, the maximum constraint time of 8,000 minutes has been replaced by the total number of RAM chips available, which is 25,000 units.

Exhibit 4.19 shows the optimum utilization of the 20,000 available RAM chips, resulting in a substantial profit. However, the previous constrained resource still exists in the production facility (though it is now the secondary constraint, following the primary constraint of the RAM chips). The secondary constraint may not be able to produce the product mix suggested by this model, if the newly revised mix requires

Product Name	Throughput $/Minute of Constraint	Required Constraint Usage (minutes)	Units of Scheduled Production	Constraint Utilization (minutes)	Throughput per Product
1. 19" Color television	$16.22	2	500/500	1,000	$ 16,220
2. 42" Plasma television	3.00	20	400/400	8,000	24,000
3. 50" High definition TV	1.94	32	150/150	4,800	9,312
4. 32" LCD television	1.13	40	155/350	6,200	7,006
		Total planned RAM chip use		20,000	—
		RAM chips avilable		20,000	—
		Throughput total			$ 56,538
		Operating expense total			47,900
		Profit			$ 8,638
		Profit percentage			15.3%
		Investment			$320,000
		Return on investment*			32.4%

*Annualized

EXHIBIT 4.19 THE RAW MATERIAL CONSTRAINT DECISION

too many minutes of production time. Consequently, it is useful to first run the throughput model based on the raw material shortage, and then test it against the traditional throughput model that is based on available minutes of production time (which is shown in Exhibit 4.20).

Thus, we see that the first model in Exhibit 4.19 reveals the most profitable usage of RAM chips, but only subject to the manufacturing constraints shown in the second model in Exhibit 4.20, which yields a significantly less satisfactory profitability outcome.

Product Name	Throughput $/Minute of Constraint	Required Constraint Usage (minutes)	Units of Scheduled Production	Constraint Utilization (minutes)	Throughput per Product
1. 19" Color television	$8.11	4	500/500	2,000	$ 16,220
2. 42" Plasma television	5.00	12	400/400	4,800	24,000
3. 50" High definition TV	6.21	10	120/150	1,200	7,452
4. 32" LCD television	7.50	6	0/350	0	0
		Total planned constraint time		8,000	—
		Maximum constraint time		8,000	—
		Throughput total			$ 47,672
		Operating expense total			47,900
		Profit			$ (228)
		Profit percentage			(0.5)%
		Investment			$320,000
		Return on investment*			(0.9)%

*Annualized

EXHIBIT 4.20 MATCHING OF PRIMARY TO SECONDARY CONSTRAINT SOLUTIONS

THE CONSTRAINT IN THE MARKETPLACE DECISION

If a company pays sufficient attention to the management of its constrained resource, it may find that it can produce all possible orders. In this case, the constraint has shifted to the marketplace, where the company must now extend its sales and marketing efforts in order to increase sales. When the constraint shifts to the marketplace, there is no longer a need to sort the throughput model by throughput per minute of the constraint (since there is no in-house constraint). Instead, we compare products based on the total throughput generated per unit. This concept is illustrated in Exhibit 4.21, where the total throughput per unit is now listed in the second column, the required constraint usage and constraint utilization columns are blank, and all potential orders are processed for all products.

When the potential exists to gain a sale, the only decision point is whether any additional operating expenses or investment required to obtain the order will be adequately offset by the increased throughput. For example, the company learns that it can sell an additional 250 42-inch plasma televisions, but only if it adds a staff person in each of the second and third shifts to handle customer queries. The two additional employees will cost $10,000 per month. The scenario is modeled in Exhibit 4.22, where the operating expense is increased by $10,000 and the scheduled production volume for the plasma television is increased from 400 to 650 units.

Product Name	Total Throughput per Unit	Required Constraint Usage (minutes)	Units of Scheduled Production	Constraint Utilization (minutes)	Throughput per Product
1. 50" High definition TV	62.10	—	150/150	—	$ 9,315
2. 42" Plasma television	60.00	—	400/400	—	24,000
3. 32" LCD television	45.00	—	350/350	—	15,750
4. 19" Color television	32.44	—	500/500	—	16,220
			Throughput total		$ 65,285
			Operating expense total		47,900
			Profit		$ 17,385
			Profit percentage		26.6%
			Investment		$320,000
			Return on investment*		65.2%

*Annualized

EXHIBIT 4.21 THROUGHPUT MODEL USED WHEN CONSTRAINT IS IN THE MARKETPLACE

Product Name	Total Throughput per Unit	Required Constraint Usage (minutes)	Units of Scheduled Production	Constraint Utilization (minutes)	Throughput per Product
1. 50" High definition TV	$62.10	—	150/150	—	$ 9,315
2. 42" Plasma television	60.00	—	650/650	—	39,000
3. 32" LCD television	45.00	—	350/350	—	15,750
4. 19" Color television	32.44	—	500/500	—	16,220
			Throughput total		$ 80,285
			Operating expense total		57,900
			Profit		$ 22,385
			Profit percentage		27.9%
			Investment		$320,000
			Return on investment*		83.9%

*Annualized

EXHIBIT 4.22   THROUGHPUT MODEL USED WHEN CONSTRAINT IS IN THE MARKETPLACE

The exhibit shows that the resulting throughput gain of $15,000 easily offsets the incremental cost increase of $10,000. Consequently, this proposal should be accepted.

THE PLANT CLOSING DECISION

Throughput modeling can be used to evaluate the decision to close an entire production facility. A common mistake is for the corporate headquarters staff to allocate the cost of shared services and general corporate overhead to a production facility, and then base the cancellation decision on the cost of both allocated overhead and the variable costs of running the facility. The key point in determining which costs to include in the plant closing decision is—would the allocated corporate expenses be reduced if the plant were to be closed? If this is not the case, then the closing decision should not include the allocated overhead. Otherwise, a plant with positive throughput could be closed, resulting in a larger net loss for the company as a whole.

This concept is illustrated in Exhibits 4.23 through 4.25. In the first exhibit, Mega Corporation has allocated the cost of shared services and general corporate overhead to each of its four divisions. The shared service allocation is based on service usage, while the allocation of general corporate expenses is based on the proportion of throughput dollars generated. Each of the divisions creates positive throughput, but the cost of the additional expenses results in the reporting of only modest profits for divisions A and B, breakeven for division C, and a clear loss for division D.

A more accurate view of the situation would have been to only allocate the cost of variable shared services expenses, which were shown in the third column of the preceding exhibit. If a division were to be closed, these expenses would also be eliminated, and so are relevant to the closing decision. The revised exhibit is shown in Exhibit 4.23, where it is readily apparent that all of the divisions have positive throughput after only variable overhead expenses are deducted.

Division	Throughput	Variable Shared Services Allocation	Fixed Shared Services Allocation	Corporate Overhead Allocation	Profit (or Loss)
A	$3,500,000	$ 590,000	$ 950,000	$1,730,000	$230,000
B	2,900,000	420,000	680,000	1,430,000	370,000
C	1,200,000	220,000	390,000	590,000	0
D	500,000	260,000	380,000	250,000	(390,000)
Totals	$8,100,000	$1,490,000	$2,400,000	$4,000,000	$210,000

EXHIBIT 4.23 OVERHEAD COST ALLOCATIONS TO DIVISIONS OF MEGA CORPORATION

Division	Throughput	Variable Shared Services Allocation	Profit (or Loss)
A	$3,500,000	$ 590,000	$2,910,000
B	2,900,000	420,000	2,480,000
C	1,200,000	220,000	980,000
D	500,000	260,000	240,000
Totals	$8,100,000	$1,490,000	$6,610,000

EXHIBIT 4.24 OVERHEAD COST ALLOCATIONS TO DIVISIONS OF MEGA CORPORATION

Division	Throughput	Variable Shared Services Allocation	Fixed Shared Services Allocation	Corporate Overhead Allocation	Profit (or Loss)
A	$3,500,000	$ 590,000	$1,130,000	$1,850,000	$(70,000)
B	2,900,000	420,000	810,000	1,520,000	150,000
C	1,200,000	220,000	460,000	630,000	(110,000)
D	—	—	—	—	—
Totals	$8,100,000	$1,490,000	$2,400,000	$4,000,000	$(30,000)

EXHIBIT 4.25 IMPACT OF PLANT CLOSURE ON TOTAL PROFITABILITY

Based on the reported loss in Exhibit 4.23, Mega Corporation's president decides to close division D. The results are shown in Exhibit 4.25.

The exhibit shows that the closure decision has eliminated $260,000 of variable shared services expenses, but the remaining overhead costs are *not* eliminated, and must now be allocated among three divisions instead of four. The result is that because of the additional overhead charges, divisions A and C both report a loss. If the same logic used to close division D is used, this would then result in the closure of divisions A and C, followed later by division B when all overhead costs are allocated to it in the absence of the other divisions.

Thus, the correct decision model would have been to only evaluate divisions based on their own throughput, less any clearly variable corporate overhead charges. Any allocation of additional costs only yields a misinterpretation of the underlying profitability of each division.

UNDERLYING CONCEPTS OF THE THROUGHPUT ANALYSIS MODEL

Though the throughput analysis model presented in this chapter seems simple enough, one should have some knowledge of its underpinnings to ensure that it is not misused. Here are some modeling issues to consider:

- *Throughput per minute is more important than total product throughput.* The model ranks products with high throughput per minute as being more important than a product having higher total throughput. Though this may at first seem counterintuitive, an emphasis on higher throughput per minute results in higher company-wide profits, because the constrained resource now has more time available to create more products with more throughput. If the model emphasized total throughput per product instead, then it could result in a strong emphasis on sales of a product requiring considerable constraint time, thereby yielding lower production unit volumes and lower profits. Thus, it can make sense to produce more of a lower-throughput item, if the lower-throughput item requires less time at the constrained resource. However, the importance of throughput per minute of constraint vanishes if the constraint shifts to the marketplace (since there is no longer an in-house constraint), at which point products should be ranked based on their total throughput per unit.

- *Dependent on identification of the constraint.* It is critical that the correct operation be identified as the actual constraint, because this drives the throughput per minute prioritization function of the model. If the wrong operation is used as the constraint, then it is likely that the wrong product mix will be scheduled for production, resulting in suboptimal throughput and profits. This also makes it important to constantly track not only the location of the constraint, but also the actual amount of constraint minutes available, which will vary over time in accordance with a variety of management decisions.

- *Batch sizing is ignored.* The model does not overtly take into account the time required to set up machines for customer-specific jobs. This can be a factor if a customer places an inordinately small order, since the setup time may exceed the run time. It is assumed that the model user will add to the throughput model the number of minutes required on the constraint for such small orders, which should include both the setup time and run time. If large setup times are needed for non-constrained workstations, then this time is not considered necessary to the decision to accept the order, since non-constrained resources are expected to have significant levels of excess production time available.

- *Less emphasis on incremental changes in operating expenses.* The model appears to be primarily configured to deal with changes in production volume and mix, with operating expenses being treated as an afterthought, since it is only listed as a single line item. The model is laid out in this manner because we do not try to correlate production volume with operating expenses. Instead, all operating expenses are summarized in one place, representing the company's total cost of capacity. If a change in operating expenses is required as part of a decision, then the person using the model should alter the operating expenses line item by the amount of the expected expense change.

- *Assumes fixed operating expenses.* The model assumes that the company's existing operating expenses will be adequate for an infinite amount of production. Though production can certainly fluctuate to some extent with no change in operating expenses, production levels will eventually increase to the point where additional operating expenses must be incurred to accommodate the increase. When this happens, the operating expenses have essentially become the new constraint, so additional expenses must then be included in the model.

- *Optimizes the entire system.* The throughput model does not initially appear to solve for total company profits or return on investment, only the correct way to handle small, localized decisions. However, because the model is centered on the appropriate use of the constrained resource, any recommended solution it generates will also be the correct decision for the company as a whole, because the entire company's results are also driven by the constrained resource. Thus, decisions based on the throughput model will not just be locally optimized; rather, they will be optimized for the company as a whole.

The user of the throughput model should be well versed in the preceding concepts in order to obtain accurate results from the model.

SUMMARY

The throughput analysis model used so extensively in this chapter appears to be a quite simple model, and yet can yield surprisingly accurate results that assist management in determining the correct course of action for many types of pricing, staffing, costing, investment, and production decisions. The model only works properly if the constrained resource has been correctly identified; otherwise, incorrect production scheduling decisions will yield suboptimal throughput and profits. Also, the model user must be aware of incremental changes in operating expenses and invested funds that are associated with each decision, and incorporate these changes into the model in order to obtain accurate results.

5

THROUGHPUT IN THE BUDGETING AND CAPITAL BUDGETING PROCESS

The typical budgeting process is designed to give management an overview of the probable structure of revenue and expenses during the upcoming year, as well as to plan for capital purchases during that period. This chapter addresses how the budget model can be modified to align it with throughput accounting concepts in the areas of capital budgeting, revenue planning, expense planning, new product introductions, direct labor planning, and the sales department.

CAPITAL BUDGETING WITH THROUGHPUT ACCOUNTING

A solid knowledge of throughput accounting concepts can go a long ways toward the avoidance of unnecessary investments, because it focuses attention on what investments will improve total company throughput or reduce operating expenses. As we will see in this section, most other capital purchase requests not impacting these areas should be declined.

The traditional capital budgeting approach involves having the management team review a series of unrelated requests from throughout the company, each one asking for funding for various projects. Management decides whether to fund each request based on the discounted cash flows projected for each one. If there are not sufficient funds available for all requests having positive discounted cash flows, then those with the largest cash flows or highest percentage returns are usually accepted first, until the funds run out.

There are several problems with this type of capital budgeting. First and most important, there is no consideration of how each requested project fits into the entire system of production—instead, most requests involve the local optimization of specific work centers that may not contribute to the total throughput of the company. Second, there is no consideration of the constrained resource, so managers cannot tell which funding requests will result in an improvement to the efficiency of that operation. Third, managers tend to engage in a great deal of speculation regarding the budgeted cash flows resulting from their requests, resulting in inaccurate discounted cash flow projections. Since many requests involve unverifiable cash flow estimates, it is impossible to discern which projects are better than others.

A greater reliance on throughput accounting concepts eliminates most of these problems. First, the priority for funding should be placed squarely on any projects that can improve the capacity of the constrained resource, based on a comparison of the incremental additional throughput created to the incremental operating expenses and investment incurred.

Second, any investment requests not involving the constrained resource should be subject to an intensive critical review, likely resulting in their rejection. Since they do not impact the constrained resource, these investments cannot impact system throughput in any way, so their sole remaining justification must be the reduction of operating expenses or the mitigation of some type of risk.

The one exception to investing in non-constrained resources is when there is so little excess capacity in a work center that it has difficulty recovering from downtime. This can be a major problem if the lack of capacity constantly causes holes in the inventory buffer, and places the constrained resource in danger of running out of work. In this case, a good investment alternative is to invest in a sufficient amount of additional sprint capacity to ensure that the system can rapidly recover from a reasonable level of downtime. If a manager is applying for a capital investment based on this reasoning, he should attach to the proposal a chart showing the capacity level at which the targeted resource has been operating over the past few months, as well as the severity of holes in the buffer caused by that operation.

At what point should a company invest in more of the constrained resource? In many cases, the company has specifically designated a resource to be its constraint, because it is so expensive to add additional capacity, so this decision is not to be taken lightly. The decision process is to review the impact on the incremental change in throughput caused by the added investment, less any changes in operating expenses. Because this type of investment represents a considerable step cost (where costs and/or the investment will jump considerably as a result of the decision), management must usually make its decision based on the perceived level of long-term throughput changes, rather than smaller expected short-term throughput increases.

The issues noted above have been addressed in the summary-level capital budgeting form shown in Exhibit 5.1. This form splits capital budgeting requests into three categories: 1. constraint-related, 2. risk-related, 3. non–constraint-related. The risk-related category covers all capital purchases for which the company must meet a legal requirement, or for which there is a perception that the company is subject to an undue amount of risk if it does *not* invest in an asset. All remaining requests that do not clearly call into the constraint-related or risk-related categories drops into a catch-all category at the bottom of the form. The intent of this format is to clearly differentiate between different types of approval requests, with each one requiring different types of analysis and management approval.

The approval levels vary significantly in the throughput-based capital request form. Approvals for constraint-related investments include a process analyst (who verifies that the request will actually impact the constraint), as well as generally higher-dollar approval levels for lower-level managers—the intent is to make it easier to approve capital requests that will improve the constrained resource. Approvals for risk-related projects first require the joint approval of the corporate attorney and chief risk officer, with added approvals for large expenditures. Finally, the approvals for non-constraint-related purchases involve lower-dollar approval levels, so the approval process is intentionally made more difficult.

Capital Request Form

Project name: _____

Name of project sponsor: _____

Submission date: _____   Project number: _____

☐ **Constraint-Related Project**	Approvals
Initial expenditure: $ _____	All _____ Process Analyst
Additional annual expenditure: $ _____	$100,000 _____ Supervisor
Impact on throughput: $ _____	
Impact on operating expenses: $ _____	$100,001– $1,000,000 _____ President
Impact on ROI: $ _____	
(Attach calculations)	$1,000,000+ _____ Board of Directors

☐ **Risk-Related Project**	Approvals
Initial expenditure: $ _____	<$50,000 { _____ Corporate Attorney
Additional annual expenditure: $ _____	_____ Chief Risk Officer
Description of legal requirement fulfilled or risk issue mitigated (attach description as needed):	$50,001+ _____ President
_____	
_____	$1,000,000+ _____ Board of Directors

☐ **Non–Constraint-Related Project**	Approvals
Initial expenditure: $ _____	All _____ Process Analyst
Additional annual expenditure: $ _____	<$10,000 _____ Supervisor
☐ Improves sprint capacity? Attach justification of sprint capacity increase	$10,001– $100,000 _____ President
☐ Other request Attach justification for other request type	$100,000+ _____ Board of Directors

---

EXHIBIT 5.1   THE THROUGHPUT-BASED CAPITAL REQUEST FORM

Once approved as part of the budgeting process, capital requests can be segregated in the budget into the three categories just noted. The basic format of this portion of the budget is shown in Exhibit 5.2.

The capital budget example shows more expenditures for risk-related projects, but in most cases the bulk of funding should be focused squarely on constraint-related projects, with only minimal funding reserved for non-constraint-related projects.

Also, the example contains an additional section at the bottom, in which is listed the incremental additional capacity of the constrained resource resulting from the new investments. In this section, the new capacity is listed with a time delay, so that a capital expenditure is fully installed before the resulting capacity is assumed to be available. Though most of the budget contains nothing but financial information, this operational information may have an impact on the company's ability to increase its sales later in the budget period, and so is extremely useful reference information.

Several examples of the capital budget decision-making process will be presented in Chapter 6, Throughput and Generally Accepted Accounting Principles.

BUDGETING FOR REVENUE WITH THROUGHPUT ACCOUNTING

In a traditional budget, the entire budget model is driven by the revenue forecast, as this information is needed to derive materials purchases, inventory and staffing levels, and operating expenses. The revenue forecast is usually summarized in one of two ways: either by total revenue dollars for each product, or by total revenue dollars by customer (which is more common when dealing with labor hour billings).

Though a valid way to obtain top-line revenue projections, this information lacks any clear linkage to directly variable costs, so managers cannot tell from the revenue budget alone how revenue projections will impact profitability. In addition, it does not show the impact of sales projections on the company's capacity constraint. A better approach is to use throughput accounting to develop a throughput forecast, either by product or by customer, that clearly shows the impact on both profits and the capacity constraint.

Capital Budget					
	1st Quarter	2nd Quarter	3rd Quarter	4th Quarter	Total
Constraint-related projects:					
Additional metal press	$500,000				$ 500,000
Refurbish old metal press			75,000		75,000
Conveyors into metal press		180,000			180,000
Subtotal	$500,000	$ 180,000	$ 75,000	$ 0	$ 755,000
Risk-related projects:					
Smokestack scrubber		850,000			850,000
Water filtration			175,000		175,000
Asbestos abatement				250,000	250,000
Subtotal	$ 0	$ 850,000	$175,000	$250,000	$1,275,000
Non-constraint-related projects:					
Automated stock carver			147,000		147,000
Paint booth replacement		263,000			263,000
Lamination department conveyors				82,000	82,000
Subtotal	$ 0	$ 263,000	$147,000	$82,000	$ 492,000
Grand Total	$500,000	$1,293,000	$397,000	$332,000	$2,522,000

EXHIBIT 5.2 THE THROUGHPUT-BASED CAPITAL BUDGET

		Incremental Improvement in Constraint Minutes		
	1st Quarter	**2nd Quarter**	**3rd Quarter**	**4th Quarter**
Operational impacts:				
Additional metal press		299,520	299,520	299,520
Refurbish old metal press				42,500
Conveyors into metal press			2,860	2,860
Total	0	299,520	302,380	344,880

EXHIBIT 5.2 CONTINUED

Exhibit 5.3 shows a traditional revenue forecast for several products, followed by a revised forecast that reveals the individual and cumulative throughput levels for the same products and product quantities shown in the original forecast.

The traditional product revenue budget shown at the top of Exhibit 5.3 presents the usual itemization of estimated product sales that many of us are accustomed to seeing. However, this view has serious shortcomings when compared to the much richer set of information listed in the bottom half of the exhibit for throughput-based information. The later portion of the exhibit reveals that the company is incapable of meeting its revenue budget, because there is not a sufficient amount of capacity available (based on 260 working days, at three shifts, assuming 80 percent efficiency) to meet its sales goals. A traditional budget would not have flagged this constraint problem anywhere, so the company would have constructed a fundamentally unsound budget and proceeded to implement it, with an essentially guaranteed revenue shortfall being the only possible outcome.

In addition, the enhanced budget shows that the company earns the least throughput per minute on its top-of-the-line carbon and titanium bikes; depending on the marketing effect of this decision, management could elect to drop production of both bikes, thereby bringing remaining estimated bike sales within range of the constraint limitation, while minimizing the resulting negative impact on throughput. Thus, the throughput approach to the revenue budget reveals not only problems with the initial forecast, but also presents a possible solution regarding how the sales mix might be modified.

A further note on the use of the throughput-based product revenue budget is to list the same product multiple times if it is forecasted to be sold to different customers at different prices (in which case it is useful to identify the customers in the budget for each line item). This makes it easier to see the throughput per unit at each price point.

The same approach can be taken to revenue a budget that is based on sales by customer. The example shown in Exhibit 5.4 assumes that sales are based on billable hours to customers.

The traditional revenue budgeting model shown in Exhibit 5.4 shows an estimate of revenues by customer, with no additional interpretive information. However, the throughput-based version at the bottom of

Traditional Product Revenue Budget:

Product Name	Unit Sales	Price/Each	Extended Revenue
1-speed road bike	2,850	$ 250	$ 712,500
3-speed road bike	5,100	$ 400	$ 2,040,000
24-speed road bike	4,800	$ 800	$ 3,840,000
24-speed carbon road bike	450	$4,000	$ 1,800,000
3-speed dual-shock mountain bike	8,750	$1,000	$ 8,750,000
24-speed titanium mountain bike	650	$2,500	$ 1,625,000
Totals	22,600		$18,767,500

Throughput-Based Product Revenue Budget:

Product Name	Unit Sales	Price/Each	Extended Revenue	Variable Cost/Unit	Throughput per Unit	Total Throughput	Constraint Time/Unit	Total Time on Constraint	Throughput per Minute
1-speed road bike	2,850	$ 250	$ 712,500	$ 70	$ 180	$ 513,000	5	14,250	$36.00
3-speed road bike	5,100	$ 400	$ 2,040,000	$ 125	$ 275	$ 1,402,500	11	56,100	$25.00
24-speed road bike	4,800	$ 800	$ 3,840,000	$ 225	$ 575	$ 2,760,000	13	62,400	$44.23
24-speed carbon road bike	450	$4,000	$ 1,800,000	$1,750	$2,250	$ 1,012,500	80	36,000	$28.13
3-speed dual-shock mountain bike	8,750	$1,000	$ 8,750,000	$ 350	$ 650	$ 5,687,500	22	192,500	$29.55
24-speed titanium mountain bike	650	$2,500	$ 1,625,000	$1,150	$1,350	$ 877,500	65	42,250	$20.77
Totals	22,600		$18,767,500			$12,253,000		403,500	

Maximum available constraint time (minutes)   299,520

EXHIBIT 5.3 VIEWS OF THE PRODUCT-BASED REVENUE BUDGET

Traditional Customer Revenue Budget:

Customer Name	Billable Hours	Price Hour	Extended Revenue
Amber Distribution Corporation	2,000	$125	$ 250,000
Bi-Way Valve Specialties	8,000	$ 85	$ 680,000
Breaker Breaker Radio Design	2,700	$125	$ 337,500
Hippo Weight Loss Clinics	4,100	$ 85	$ 348,500
Mining Safety Engineers	10,500	$ 65	$ 682,500
Vessel Insurance Brokers	500	$125	$ 62,500
Totals	27,800		$2,361,000

Throughput-Based Customer Revenue Budget:

Customer Name	Billable Hours	Price/ Hour	Extended Revenue	Variable Cost/Hour	Throughput per Hour	Total Throughput
Amber Distribution Corporation	2,000	$125	$ 250,000	$81.75	$43.25	$ 86,500
Bi-Way Valve Specialties	8,000	$ 85	$ 680,000	$72.35	$12.65	$101,200
Breaker Breaker Radio Design	2,700	$125	$ 337,500	$81.75	$43.25	$116,775
Hippo Weight Loss Clinics	4,100	$ 85	$ 348,500	$72.35	$12.65	$ 51,865
Mining Safety Engineers	10,500	$ 65	$ 682,500	$66.50	–$ 1.50	–$ 15,750
Vessel Insurance Brokers	500	$125	$ 62,500	$81.75	$43.25	$ 21,625
Totals	27,800		$2,361,000			$362,215

EXHIBIT 5.4 VIEWS OF THE CUSTOMER-BASED REVENUE BUDGET

Labor Category Aggregation	Billable Hours	Price/ Hour	Extended Revenue	Variable Cost/Hour	Throughput per Hour	Total Throughput	Staff Required*	Staff Available
Expert Consultant	5,200	125	$ 650,000	$ 81.75	$43.25	$224,900	3.1	2
Senior Consultant	12,100	85	$1,028,500	$ 72.35	$12.65	$153,065	7.3	7
Junior Consultant	10,500	65	$ 682,500	$ 66.50	–$ 1.50	–$ 15,750	6.3	4
	27,800		$2,361,000			$362,215		

*Assumes 80% billable hours

EXHIBIT 5.4 CONTINUED

the exhibit reveals a great deal more information. When variable costs (in this case, labor) are subtracted from the budgeted revenue to arrive at throughput, we find that there is a loss on the work being done for the Mining Safety Engineers customer, which may prompt a discussion of re-pricing this work or of dropping the customer. In addition, the model then summarizes the labor used in the various customer projects by labor category and calculates the amount of staffing required, based on the estimate of billable hours and an 80 percent billable percentage for each employee. This information tells management that it must hire additional staff in several labor categories in order to have sufficient staff to meet its revenue budget.

If a company could accumulate information about the blended throughput dollars and constraint times being used for individual customers, it could enter this information into the customer-based revenue budget, thereby giving insights into which customers could be dropped in order to meet a capacity constraint; however, this information is more difficult to accumulate, and also assumes that customers will continue to purchase the same product mix in the future, which can be extremely difficult to estimate.

BUDGETING FOR NEW PRODUCTS WITH THROUGHPUT ACCOUNTING

A traditional budgeting model will usually include the impact of a new product introduction by listing it in a product-based revenue budget such as the one shown at the top of Exhibit 5.3. However, each product introduction needs to include the resulting additional impact on the constrained resource, using the model at the bottom of Exhibit 5.3. If this additional information is not obtained, then management has no idea if a supposedly profitable new product will actually require so much constraint time that it eliminates the production of other products that could have created more throughput per minute of constraint time.

If the constraint is in the market, then the only issue with a new product introduction is whether the added investment and any incremental change in operating expenses are adequately offset by the increased throughput.

BUDGETING FOR OPERATING EXPENSES WITH THROUGHPUT ACCOUNTING

The main reason for a budget is to give management a model of how the company should operate during the budget period, based on the impact of operational and financial changes that management wants to implement during the budget period. However, the traditional budget model is designed to show results based on the local optimization of resources rather than system-wide resources, which usually results in counterproductive budgeting decisions. For example, if expenses are projected to be too high, management may mandate an across-the-board 10 percent budget cut for all departments, which will likely reduce both the capacity of the constrained resource and shrink operating expenses to such an extent that the ability of the entire system to support the current level of throughput has now been reduced. To avoid this scenario, the budget model must be altered to present information in a throughput accounting format that more clearly shows the impact of budgetary changes on the ability of the entire system to generate throughput.

Unfortunately, it is very difficult to create a quantitative format for how a change in operating expenses will impact total system throughput, since in many cases there does not appear to be a direct or even an indirect link between some costs and the generation of throughput. Consequently, the creation of a budget where expenses support throughput generation requires an extremely detailed knowledge of how the entire system works together to create throughput.

In many cases where no link between an expense and throughput can be found, management is still able to wield a sharp budgeting axe in cutting expenses. Thus, there are considerable differences in how various budget line items should be treated, based on their impact on throughput. Any expense supporting throughput should only be cut after detailed review by a process analyst, while other expenses can be cut with much less review. This interpretation of the budget model results in a change in the budgeting format, which is shown in Exhibit 5.5. The exhibit shows a before-and-after department budget where the first version ignores the impact of throughput, while the second version splits operating expenses into those impacting throughput

	1st Quarter	2nd Quarter	3rd Quarter	4th Quarter	Total
		Version 1:			
Bank fees	3,000	4,500	2,500	4,000	14,000
Legal fees	15,000	18,500	32,000	19,000	84,500
Promotional materials	82,000	0	48,000	28,500	158,500
Salaries, accounting	85,000	87,000	87,000	91,000	350,000
Salaries, corporate	105,000	110,000	143,000	141,000	499,000
Salaries, engineering	190,000	200,000	203,000	205,000	798,000
Salaries, marketing	20,000	21,000	21,000	22,000	84,000
Salaries, production	280,000	275,000	285,000	290,000	1,130,000
Salaries, sales	150,000	175,000	180,000	195,000	700,000
Supplies	17,500	16,000	13,500	19,000	66,000
Taxes, payroll	65,155	68,138	72,142	74,104	279,539
Trade shows	0	100,000	0	0	100,000
Travel and entertainment	10,500	14,500	17,000	12,000	54,000
Total	1,023,155	1,089,638	1,104,142	1,100,604	4,317,539

	1st Quarter	2nd Quarter	3rd Quarter	4th Quarter	Total
		Version 2:			
Not Throughput-Related:					
Promotional materials	82,000	0	48,000	28,500	158,500
Salaries, engineering	190,000	200,000	203,000	205,000	798,000
Salaries, marketing	20,000	21,000	21,000	22,000	84,000
Salaries, production	280,000	275,000	285,000	290,000	1,130,000
Salaries, sales	150,000	175,000	180,000	195,000	700,000
Trade shows	0	100,000	0	0	100,000
Travel and entertainment	8,000	10,000	16,000	6,000	40,000
Subtotal	730,000	781,000	753,000	746,500	3,010,500
Not Throughput-Supportive:					
Bank fees	3,000	4,500	2,500	4,000	14,000
Legal fees	15,000	18,500	32,000	19,000	84,500
Salaries, accounting	85,000	87,000	87,000	91,000	350,000
Salaries, corporate	105,000	110,000	143,000	141,000	499,000
Supplies	17,500	16,000	13,500	19,000	66,000
Taxes, payroll	65,155	68,138	72,142	74,104	279,539
Travel and entertainment	2,500	4,500	1,000	6,000	14,000
Subtotal	293,155	308,638	351,142	354,104	1,307,039

EXHIBIT 5.5   BEFORE-AND-AFTER THROUGHPUT EXPENSE BUDGET

and those that do not. The expenses in the second version can be shifted between the two categories based on whether they affect the company's throughput capacity.

However, the exhibit clearly shows that *most* expenses will be attributable in some manner to throughput capacity, since most corporate expenses involve departments that are directly related to the production of revenue, such as engineering, production, marketing, and sales. Only such classic overhead expenses as accounting, general corporate costs, and legal expenses can be reduced with some assurance that the reductions will not impact throughput.

The discovery that most operating expenses impact throughput in some way does not mean that managers are not allowed to take a paring knife to various throughput-related expenses, however. If expense reduction were entirely forbidden, then any new expense allowed into the corporate cost structure would essentially be retained forever. However, it does mean that changes in some expense categories must be made with a detailed knowledge of their eventual impact on throughput.

It may be necessary to employ a process analyst as part of the budget team, just to obtain verification from an independent expert of how a budgeted cost change will alter a company's throughput capacity.

Thus far, the discussion of operating expenses has primarily focused on a company's ability to cut expenses. However, how should the budgeting process handle requests for *increased* operating expenses? The primary guideline should be that the existing level of operating expenses be sufficient to handle not only existing but also any projected increases in throughput. If not, then some elements of operating expenses become the constraint, at which point increases in those expenses should be included in the budget. As previously noted for expense reductions, any expense increases of this type should be reviewed by a process analyst who can determine their impact on a company's throughput capacity.

BUDGETING FOR PRODUCTION LABOR EXPENSES WITH THROUGHPUT ACCOUNTING

The standard ways to budget for production staffing levels are to
1. incrementally adjust existing staffing levels based on forecasted

revenue changes, or 2. to extrapolate labor requirements derived by multiplying the forecasted revenue for the budget period by the labor routings for each product listed in the forecast. Many companies start with the latter method and compare it to the results obtained from the first approach, and then adopt a hybrid solution. These techniques will yield reasonably accurate staffing levels for a company attempting to create locally optimized manufacturing operations. However, they will likely result in inadequate staffing levels when capacity constraints are taken into account.

When throughput is taken into account, it is necessary to hire additional employees when either of the following two circumstances arise:

1. When the sprint capacity of key workstations positioned upstream from the constrained resource is insufficient to recover from system downtime to such an extent that buffers are repeatedly penetrated

2. When the constrained resource could generate more throughput with the addition of more staff

Neither of these circumstances will be highlighted by estimating labor needs from labor routing records, nor by extrapolating current staffing levels. Instead, a process analyst must investigate the reasons why deep buffer penetrations occur, and only recommend labor increases at the problem workstations if these additions will yield a significant level of additional sprint capacity. In addition, the process analyst must make a similar determination for the additional staffing of the constrained resource.

In many cases, less than one full-time equivalent position is needed to improve the capacity of the constrained resource, which means that a company will have an under-utilized employee at that location. This is fine, as long as the incremental increase in throughput caused by the addition of this employee exceeds the incremental cost of the employee.

For example, McKoy Shovels is investigating the possibility of hiring a $25/hour employee to work on its constrained resource, which is a metal bending machine. This person is only needed during machine setups, which will occupy four hours per day. As a result, the machine will be able to bend an additional 150 snow shovel blades per day, having a throughput of $2 each. This additional work will yield a throughput improvement of $300 (150 shovel blades × $2 throughput per unit), as compared to the $200 daily cost of the employee ($25/hour × 8 hours). Since the incremental throughput of $300, less $200 of additional operating expenses, results in a net profit of $100, the position should be filled.

BUDGETING FOR SALES DEPARTMENT EXPENSES WITH THROUGHPUT ACCOUNTING

It is entirely possible that the constrained resource is not in the production area or the marketplace at all (the two most common areas) but rather in the sales department. This problem is most evident when the company's sales funnel begins with a large number of prospective sales, but narrows down to a small number of completed sales due to a bottleneck somewhere in the sales conversion process. The identification of the constrained resource within the sales funnel can be determined as part of the budgeting process, usually with an analysis similar to the one shown in Exhibit 5.6.

The exhibit shows the basic steps needed to advance through the sales funnel, from initial identification of the customer through closing the deal. For each step, the table shows the actual time used on various steps in the process, as compared to the theoretical amount of staff capacity available for each step. The table reveals that the constrained resource is the needs assessment, for which the actual

Steps in Sales Funnel	Actual Time Used (hours)	Theoretical Capacity (hours)
Initial identification	450	700
Customer qualification	120	240
Needs assessment	300	300
Letter of understanding	50	80
Product demonstration	620	800
Solution proposal	2,400	3,100
Negotiation	280	400
Closing	100	200

EXHIBIT 5.6   SALES FUNNEL BOTTLENECK IDENTIFICATION

time used has matched the theoretical maximum available. Thus, for budgeting purposes, management should bolster the ranks of the sales engineers who are responsible for creating needs assessments.

If a company does not perform this analysis, then it may budget for increases in the wrong types of sales positions, which will yield no new sales if the additions do not address the constraint.

SUMMARY

Capital budgeting decisions in a throughput environment focus on investments in just those areas that impact the capacity constraint, with most other investment proposals being rejected. The primary role of the accountant in this new capital budgeting process is to identify the constrained capacity for which an investment is being requested and the necessity for the additional capacity, as well as analyze the projected impact on throughput. This varies considerably from the accountant's traditional role of ensuring that all parts of the capital request form are completed, and perhaps investigating some of the assumptions included in the form.

Throughput accounting plays a similarly key role in the annual budgeting process, especially in the identification of how various types of revenue will generate throughput and impact the constrained resource. Thus, the accountant should be instrumental in modifying the budget model to provide the key throughput and constraint information that will help a company meet its budgeted goals.

6

THROUGHPUT AND GENERALLY ACCEPTED ACCOUNTING PRINCIPLES

If a company were to use throughput accounting, it would obtain somewhat different results than would be the case if it used generally accepted accounting principles. This chapter explains the differences between the two systems and how they can be reconciled through the use of additional general ledger accounts and modified financial statement layouts.

THE NATURE OF GENERALLY ACCEPTED ACCOUNTING PRINCIPLES

Generally accepted accounting principles (GAAP) are the rules and regulations promulgated by a variety of accounting organizations, including the Financial Accounting Standards Board and the American Society of Certified Public Accountants, as well as such predecessor organizations as the Committee on Accounting Procedure and the Accounting Principles Board. Their GAAP rulings are contained within a variety of technical documents that include Statements of Financial Accounting Standards, Interpretations, Opinions, Technical Bulletins, Statements of Position, Emerging Issues Task Force Positions, Industry Guides, Practice Bulletins, and Implementation Guides. This multitude of rules and regulations is summarized in the *Wiley GAAP Guide*, which is reissued annually by John Wiley & Sons.

The definition of GAAP is well stated in the *Wiley GAAP Guide*, as follows:

> Generally Accepted Accounting Principles are concerned with the measurement of economic activity, the time when such measurements are to be made and recorded, the disclosures surrounding this activity, and the preparation and presentation of summarized economic information in the form of financial statements. GAAP develops when questions arise about how to best accomplish those objectives— measurement, timing of recognition, disclosure, or presentation. In response to those questions, GAAP is either prescribed in official pronouncements of authoritative bodies empowered to create it, or it originates over time through the development of customary practices that evolve when authoritative bodies fail to respond.[1]

The reason a chapter is being devoted to the differences between throughput accounting and GAAP is that GAAP requires the measurement and presentation of financial information in a manner that cannot be used for throughput accounting. Consequently, we will examine the differences between these systems of accounting and derive a reconciliation process so that financial statements constructed using GAAP can be translated into financial results that accommodate the throughput accounting system.

DIFFERENCES BETWEEN THROUGHPUT
AND GAAP ACCOUNTING

There are several areas in which throughput accounting varies from GAAP. The most important issue is that GAAP requires that overhead costs be allocated to inventory, which in turn may or may not be charged to expenses in the current period. This is done under the assumption that operating expenses incurred during the current period are related to any inventory produced during that period, and so can be associated with that inventory until such time as it is sold. The applicable GAAP is contained within Chapter 4 of Accounting Research Bulletin (ARB) Number 43, which states:

---

1. Reproduced with permission, pp 1–2 of the *Wiley GAAP Guide* by Epstein, Nach, and Bragg (John Wiley & Sons, 2007).

The exclusion of all overheads from inventory costs does not constitute an accepted accounting procedure.[2]

The accounting research bulletin goes on to provide the following guidance regarding overhead allocation:

The primary basis of accounting for inventories is cost, which has been generally defined as the price paid or consideration given to acquire an asset. As applied to inventories, cost means in principle the sum of the applicable expenditures and charges directly or indirectly incurred in bringing an article to its existing condition and location ... production overheads are allocated to each unit of production on the basis of the actual use of the production facilities.[3]

Thus, GAAP clearly states that overhead must be allocated to inventory, and the failure to do so is not acceptable.

Throughput accounting takes the opposite stance that overhead costs are *not* related to inventory in any way, and so should not be allocated to inventory. Instead, operating expenses represent the cost of production capacity during a period of time, and should be charged to expense during that period.

There is another underlying difference between the two systems that is somewhat less obvious. GAAP accounting assumes that both the inventory held in storage and the overhead costs allocated to it are valuable company assets, only to be charged to expense when the inventory is sold. Under throughput accounting, the preference is to avoid the production of excess inventory because it represents an immediate use of cash (for the materials contained within the inventory), requires additional storage expenses, and can lose its value over time because of damage or obsolescence. Thus, throughput accounting assumes that inventory is to be avoided, which is a common characteristic of a liability.

Another difference between the systems is the treatment of direct labor expenses. Under GAAP, direct labor is assumed to be directly related to the incremental production of inventory, and its cost is therefore assigned to inventory. This means that, as was the case with overhead costs, direct labor can be stored as an asset across multiple accounting periods, and

---

2. Accounting Research Board Bulletin No. 43, Chapter 4, "Inventory Pricing"
3. Ibid.

will only be charged to expense when the inventory is sold. Throughput accounting holds that direct labor is very similar to other overhead costs in that it really represents the cost of production capacity, and so should be charged to expense in the current period.

The different treatment by the two accounting systems of expense allocation to inventory can have an impact on performance reward systems. Under GAAP, a manager knows that overproduction of inventory will shift some direct labor and other operating expenses out of the current period and into the inventory asset account, thereby artificially driving up profits and making it easier to earn a bonus. However, if throughput accounting is used, these costs must be charged to the current period, so there is no incentive to create too much inventory.

There are other lesser differences between the two systems. First, the layout of a GAAP income statement specifies that direct materials, direct labor, and overhead charges be itemized under the cost of goods sold, resulting in a gross margin that includes these three costs. Throughput accounting only assumes that totally variable expenses (i.e., materials) should be included in the cost of goods sold, which results in a "throughput contribution" figure instead of a gross margin. Thus, throughput accounting will yield a much higher throughput contribution than the gross margin resulting from a GAAP presentation of the income statement. Also, a GAAP income statement would itemize all other operating expenses in a variety of expense categories, such as wages, supplies, and utilities. Under throughput accounting, there is less emphasis on this additional level of detail, so all expenses could be clumped into a single "operating expenses" line item, or broken out in varying degrees of detail, at the option of whomever is using the income statement.

INCOME STATEMENTS FOR THROUGHPUT ACCOUNTING AND GAAP

If throughput accounting were to be used for the construction of an income statement, the format and content of the statement would appear slightly different than what would be used under GAAP guidelines. It would only include direct materials in the cost of goods sold, which would result in a "throughput contribution" line item instead of a gross margin. All other costs would be lumped into an "operating expenses" category below the throughput contribution margin, yielding a net income figure at the bottom. The two versions of the income statement are shown in Exhibit 6.1.

Note that the throughput contribution will always be substantially higher than the gross margin used under GAAP reporting, because throughput accounting assumes that direct labor and overhead expenses are part of operating expenses, not the cost of goods sold. Also, the income statement format used for throughput accounting could separate the various operating expenses into line items, rather than clustering this information into a single number. By doing so, management would have a better understanding of individual expenses.

	GAAP Format	Throughput Format
Sales	$8,250,000	$8,250,000
Cost of Goods Sold		
Materials	1,650,000	1,650,000
Direct Labor	825,000	
Overhead	2,050,000	
Total Cost of Goods Sold	$4,525,000	
Gross Margin	$3,725,000	
Throughput Contribution		$6,600,000
Operating Expenses		
Advertising	$ 75,000	
Commissions	50,000	
Depreciation	80,000	
Outside Services	20,000	
Salaries and Payroll Taxes	3,005,000	
Supplies	60,000	
Utilities	35,000	
Total Operating Expenses	$3,325,000	$6,200,000
Net Income	$ 400,000	$ 400,000

EXHIBIT 6.1   INCOME STATEMENT LAYOUTS USING GAAP AND THROUGHPUT ACCOUNTING

The formats in Exhibit 6.1 would also result in different net income figures if there were any change in inventory levels during the reporting period. This is because all operating expenses are charged to the current period under throughput accounting, but would be either stored in or released from inventory under GAAP, if inventory levels were to rise or fall, respectively. This issue is covered in more detail in the Reconciling Throughput Accounting to GAAP section, later in this chapter.

The balance sheet format would be the same for both throughput accounting and GAAP, though, as just noted, differences in inventory levels could alter the results appearing on it. In particular, the lack of overhead absorption in inventory, as mandated by throughput accounting, would reduce the investment in inventory appearing on the balance sheet, while any changes in net income would be reflected in the stockholders' equity section of the balance sheet.

MODIFYING THE CHART OF ACCOUNTS FOR THROUGHPUT ACCOUNTING

The typical chart of accounts constructed for GAAP accounting uses three inventory accounts, which are as follows:

Account Number	Account Name
xxxx	Raw Materials Inventory
xxxx	Work-in-Process Inventory
xxxx	Finished Goods Inventory

The raw materials inventory account includes the purchase cost of raw materials, which matches the requirements of a throughput system. However, the work-in-process inventory and finished goods inventory accounts also include an overhead allocation that is required under GAAP. Since a throughput accounting system only wants these two accounts to contain the totally variable cost of the inventory, it is necessary to create an additional two accounts where the overhead allocations assigned to work-in-process and finished goods can be stored. This allows one to create throughput accounting reports *without* an inventory overhead allocation, as well as GAAP reports *with* an inventory overhead allocation. The resulting throughput accounting chart of accounts would therefore be as follows:

Account Number	Account Name
xxxx	Raw Materials Inventory
xxxx	Work-in-Process Inventory, Materials Only
xxxx	Work-in-Process Inventory, Overhead Only
xxxx	Finished Goods Inventory, Materials Only
xxxx	Finished Goods Inventory, Overhead Only

Most accounting software packages contain report writing modules that can use this slight modification to the chart of accounts to easily generate standard reports that can accommodate both the GAAP and throughput systems.

RECONCILING THROUGHPUT ACCOUNTING TO GAAP

Virtually all companies have accounting systems designed to follow GAAP guidelines, while throughput accounting is primarily used by the cost accounting and financial analysis staff. Therefore, since the GAAP system is already in place, it is much easier to convert the results of the existing GAAP system to throughput results, rather than do the reverse.

To do so, the total amount of all direct labor and overhead stored in inventory must be identified and removed from the inventory value listed on the balance sheet. The simplest way to do this is to identify the net change in the amount of direct labor and overhead stored in inventory during the reporting period, and recognize that change as an additional expense in the income statement. The calculation for doing so is as follows:

(Ending inventory in units) × (overhead rate per unit

+ direct labor rate per unit) − (Beginning inventory in units)

× (overhead rate per unit + direct labor rate per unit)

= Change in value of overhead and direct labor in inventory

Revenue		$2,250,000
Cost of goods sold		
Materials	$495,000	
Direct labor	315,000	
Overhead	420,000	
Total cost of goods		$1,230,000
Gross margin		1,020,000
Operating expenses		940,000
Net profit (loss)		$ 80,000

EXHIBIT 6.2   CADDYSHACK GOLF COMPANY GAAP INCOME STATEMENT

For example, the Caddyshack Golf Company uses GAAP to record the financial results shown in Exhibit 6.2 for the month of August.

In addition, Caddyshack experiences a net increase in inventory during the month, due to excessively high levels of production. The net change calculation for the amount of direct labor and overhead stored in inventory is as follows:

(24,300 ending inventory units)

$\times$ ($4.10 overhead/unit + $3.15 labor rate/unit)

= $176,175 − (10,800 beginning inventory units)

$\times$ ($4.50 overhead/unit + $3.75 direct labor rate/unit)

= $89,100

= $87,075(comprised of $51,030 overhead + $36,045 direct labor)

Note that the higher production levels during the month also resulted in lower per-unit overhead and direct labor allocations for the ending inventory.

When we strip this incremental cost allocation out of the inventory asset account in the balance sheet and move it back to the income statement, we arrive at the results shown in Exhibit 6.3.

Thus, Caddyshack has masked a throughput loss by overproducing, thereby shifting some of its current operating expenses into the inventory asset account. This information is hidden under GAAP accounting, but is readily observable when the information is restated in a throughput-based income statement.

	GAAP Format	+ Format Adjustments	+ Inventory Adjustments	= Throughput Format
Revenue	$2,250,000			$2,250,000
Cost of goods sold				
Materials	495,000			495,000
Direct labor	315,000	$ (315,000)		0
Overhead	420,000	(420,000)		0
Total cost of goods	1,230,000			495,000
Gross margin	1,020,000			
Throughput contribution				1,755,000
Operating expenses	940,000	735,000	$87,075	1,762,075
Net profit (loss)	$ 80,000	$ 0	$87,075	$ (7,075)

EXHIBIT 6.3   CADDYSHACK GOLF COMPANY THROUGHPUT INCOME STATEMENT

THROUGHPUT ACCOUNTING AND COST-PLUS CONTRACTING

In addition to GAAP, it may also be necessary for a throughput accounting system to issue reports that follow yet another set of guidelines needed for cost-plus contracts. Under a cost-plus arrangement, a company is allowed to charge a customer for the cost of all materials, labor, and overhead incurred while engaged in a project on behalf of the customer, plus some predetermined profit percentage. Cost-plus arrangements are commonly used by government entities to compensate contractors for very large construction projects, or research projects where the outcome is in such doubt that contractors refuse to be compensated under fixed-fee arrangements.

The rules for cost-plus contracts vary by contract, but the basic concept is that a very specific list of which costs may be charged—and which may *not* be charged—are included in the initial contract. The company then creates accounts for each of the expenses listed for the contract, and tracks its costs in accordance with the contract requirements. Cost-plus rules virtually require the use of absorption costing, since overhead expenses become an integral part of the product price and so must be assigned to each product.

Given the absolute need for absorption costing in cost-plus contracts, the only way to use throughput accounting in the same environment is to create a separate set of management and financial reports that charge all overhead costs to expense in the current period, and a separate set of reports for all cost-plus contracts. This may require the use of substantially more accounts than the few additional inventory accounts noted earlier in the Modifying the Chart of Accounts for Throughput Accounting section.

SUMMARY

This chapter revealed the GAAP sources that require companies to allocate overhead costs to inventory, and also showed the impact of this requirement on a company's financial results. It also covered differences in the layout of financial statements, and how to reconcile differences between the two reporting formats. Though the GAAP and throughput accounting systems will result in significantly different operational results, it is possible to use both systems with a relatively modest amount of reconciliation effort.

7

THROUGHPUT AND CONTROL SYSTEMS

The typical company installs a myriad of controls throughout its operations and accounting systems, which flag many divergences from planned performance. However, a company focusing on its constrained resource will adopt a different approach where the bulk of its controls are centered on the three chief elements of a constraint management system—1. the constrained resource, 2. the inventory buffers located in front of the constrained resource and final assembly, and 3. several aspects of the production scheduling system. Though it is still necessary to have control systems in other parts of a company (especially given the control structure imposed by the Sarbanes-Oxley Act on public companies), they are less important than controls in these three areas. This chapter describes controls that can be used to monitor the constrained resource, inventory buffers, and production scheduling.

CONSTRAINED RESOURCE CONTROLS

The central concept of constraint management is to ensure that the constrained resource is fully operational at all times. Consequently, a key control is to report on the level of constraint utilization. This is accomplished with a simple report that itemizes resource usage on a trend line, such as the one shown in Exhibit 7.1.

Though the report shown in the exhibit summarizes utilization data by week, it can also be issued on a daily basis. The reason is that production management must have a high-speed feedback loop for constraint performance in order to guard against multi-day drops in utilization that will lead to significant throughput declines.

Constrained Resource Utilization

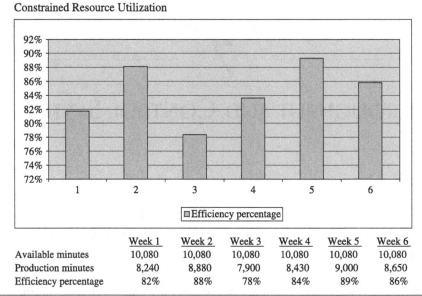

	Week 1	Week 2	Week 3	Week 4	Week 5	Week 6
Available minutes	10,080	10,080	10,080	10,080	10,080	10,080
Production minutes	8,240	8,880	7,900	8,430	9,000	8,650
Efficiency percentage	82%	88%	78%	84%	89%	86%

EXHIBIT 7.1 RESOURCE UTILIZATION REPORT

If the resource utilization report shows a low level of efficiency, the production manager's next task is to determine the cause of the problem. One metric that may provide this information is the ratio of maintenance downtime to the total available operating time of the constrained resource (which is described more fully in Chapter 8, Throughput and Performance Measurement and Reporting Systems). This measurement tracks the proportion of downtime required for maintenance activities, and should be shown on a trend line. The report will not reveal the specific work center problems that caused maintenance downtime, so the production manager will need to investigate further to determine specific causes.

A ratio similar to the ratio of maintenance downtime to the total available operating time of the constrained resource can be used for any other issue that keeps production from occurring. Among the more common reasons are shortages of materials and labor, as well as setup times. For material and labor shortages, there will likely be more detailed underlying reasons, such as a lot sizing policy that keeps materials from reaching the constraint, or a labor union rule regarding employee breaks that results in a labor shortage. Thus, the recording of the initial reason for constraint downtime may result in a wide array of solutions that may not initially appear to even be related to the metric being recorded.

One of the most subtle activities causing a loss of throughput is the scrapping of items downstream from the constraint, since the constraint time invested in each scrapped item is permanently lost. The manager in charge of the constraint itself will not even see this problem, since the loss occurs elsewhere in the plant. The extent of this problem can be measured with the "throughput of post-constraint scrap" metric, which is also described in Chapter 8. This is a more difficult metric to calculate, since one must use routing records to determine the constraint time required for each scrapped item, and summarize this information for the reporting period.

A variety of metrics have been described in this section that itemize ways in which the throughput of the constrained resource can potentially be negatively impacted. It is useful to bring this information together into a single visual representation, so the production manager can quickly determine the relative size of the various issues. An example of this format is shown in Exhibit 7.2, where 100 percent of the constraint's available time is shown in a stacked bar chart, with each problem area itemized as a separate bar, as well as in the numeric table shown below the bar chart.

Use of the measurement techniques noted in this section will inevitably lead to detailed investigation of many areas, with a multitude of solutions being implemented. While making these changes, it is important to closely link them to the metrics, so that management can see the results of their actions. Otherwise, a great deal of effort may go into a change that is presumed to enhance constraint efficiency, when in actuality, no measurable improvement results from it.

BUFFER CONTROLS

Buffer controls fall into two categories: the daily investigation of the late arrival of materials at the buffer, and the long-term determination of the correct size of the buffer. Both controls are described below.

The best single day-to-day control over buffer holes is the Buffer Management Report, which is described in detail in Chapter 8, and

Constrained Resource Efficiency

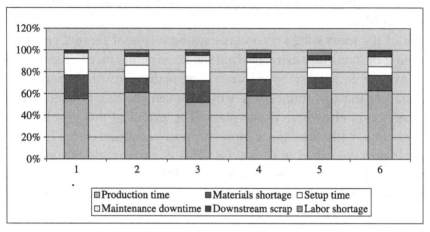

	Week 1	Week 2	Week 3	Week 4	Week 5	Week 6
Production time	55%	61%	52%	58%	65%	63%
Materials shortage	22%	13%	20%	15%	10%	14%
Setup time	15%	12%	18%	16%	9%	8%
Maintenance downtime	5%	8%	5%	4%	7%	9%
Downstream scrap	2%	3%	3%	4%	4%	5%
Labor shortage	1%	3%	2%	3%	5%	1%
Total	100%	100%	100%	100%	100%	100%

EXHIBIT 7.2   RESOURCE EFFICIENCY SUMMARIZATION REPORT

reproduced below in Exhibit 7.3. This report itemizes the precise reasons that work-in-process has arrived late at the buffer, as well as the source of the problem. Proper investigation and resolution of the reasons behind buffer holes, as shown in this report, present an excellent opportunity to ensure that production problems upstream of the buffer do not recur.

Date	Arrival Time Required	Actual Arrival Time	Originating Work Station	Cause of Delay
Sept. 11	9/11, 2 P.M.	9/12, 3 P.M.	Paint shop	Paint nozzles clogged
Sept. 14	9/14, 9 A.M.	9/16, 4 P.M.	Electrolysis	Power outage
Sept. 19	9/19, 10 A.M.	9/19, 4 P.M.	Electrolysis	Electrodes corroded
Sept. 19	9/19, 4 P.M.	9/25, 10 A.M.	Paint shop	Paint nozzles clogged
Sept. 23	9/23, 1 P.M.	9/24, 9 A.M.	Paint shop	Ran out of paint

EXHIBIT 7.3   THE BUFFER MANAGEMENT REPORT

Control over the proper sizing of a buffer does not result in the precise problem definitions just shown in the buffer management report because the correct size of the buffer is, to some degree, a matter of opinion. A possible control is to compile, on a trend line, the number of times that the expedite zone of the buffer is penetrated. The expedite zone is that portion of the buffer where a lack of inventory from an upstream work center will trigger an expediting activity to ensure that replenishment inventory arrives as soon as possible. If there is an increasing trend of expedite zone penetrations, then action should be taken to either increase the size of the buffer or to increase the amount of upstream sprint capacity at the work centers causing the penetrations. Conversely, if there is a declining trend, then it may be possible to consider a gradual reduction in the size of the buffer.

PRODUCTION SCHEDULING CONTROLS

Production scheduling is primarily concerned with the flow of materials, both into and through the production facility. Accordingly, the first two controls cited below address how this flow can be monitored. Another control addresses the matching of actual to planned production, while the final control is concerned with the monitoring of machine usage levels.

A key task of the production scheduler is to release jobs into the production process only when needed, so that they arrive at the inventory buffer at the appropriate time. If releases occur too soon, a large work-in-process buildup occurs upstream of the constraint, which can interfere with the timely completion of jobs. An appropriate control for the detection of this problem is to monitor the amount of upstream work-in-process. This can involve the dollar value of material present in the upstream area, but it may be easier to simply report on the total number of jobs present, and to do so on a trend line. This control can also be performed with a simple visual inspection of the volume of material positioned in front of the various upstream work centers.

The production scheduling process actually begins well before the release of materials into the production process, since it also relies upon the timely delivery of materials from suppliers to the company. Any delay in this area will have adverse consequences on the ability of the constraint to generate throughput, and so requires a control point to warn management of any impending problems. One possible control is the monitoring of advance shipping notices from freight carriers, so the materials management staff will know when deliveries are scheduled to arrive. Another option is either direct computer integration with supplier systems to determine the shipment dates of scheduled deliveries, or the more common approach of calling to inquire about deliveries on a regular basis. At a minimum, this level of monitoring is certainly required for any materials whose absence could shut down the constraint.

A major problem can arise when the constraint manager elects to run excessively long production runs at the constraint in order to achieve a higher level of efficiency than may have been scheduled into the production plan. This results in some amount of production going to inventory rather than to customers. To detect this issue, always compare the production quantities scheduled at the constrained resource to the amounts produced. If the actual production levels are persistently high by significant amounts, it is likely that the constraint manager is intentionally padding his work center efficiency numbers at the cost of an additional corporate investment in inventory.

Production scheduling is highly dependent on the ability of work centers to operate at expected levels of efficiency and duration, or else scheduled jobs will not be completed on time. Thus, a key control is for the scheduling staff to monitor actual work center production levels, not only for the constrained resource, but everywhere in the facility. By doing so, the staff will have some idea of declines in production levels that may impact scheduled production. However, this is a historical analysis that gives no indication of forthcoming project work center downtime, so it is also necessary for the production scheduling staff to be in close communication with the maintenance manager, or to at least have access to the maintenance work schedule, to determine which work centers are scheduled for maintenance downtime. They can then use this information to reschedule production around any temporary bottlenecks in the production process, thereby mitigating any excessively negative impact on throughput.

SUMMARY

The control points noted in this chapter are critical to the proper functioning of a constraint management system, since they flag problems occurring at the constrained resource, at the inventory buffers, and at various points in the production scheduling process. As long as management reacts promptly to any flagged problems revealed by the control system, throughput levels should remain high.

The data entry work required to create many of the controls noted in this chapter can itself lead to reduced efficiency levels. This is because the people collecting the information used in the controls may also be primarily responsible for the operation of the constraint management system, and the data collection takes time away from their primary task. To avoid this loss of focus, have an ancillary support person collect the information, or simplify the data collection task, or use automated data collection systems.

In Chapter 8 we turn to the discussion of a number of performance metrics and reports, some of which were alluded to in this chapter as being key components of an effective control system.

8

THROUGHPUT AND PERFORMANCE MEASUREMENT AND REPORTING SYSTEMS

A traditional set of performance metrics and reports cause managers to focus their attention in a multitude of areas, rather than on the constrained resource, and so should be largely avoided. The proper use of a constraint-based management system requires the use of an entirely different set of supporting performance measurement and reporting systems. The key concept behind this new system is to use a measurement or report that focuses only on the performance of the corporate production system as a whole, with the measurement of localized performance optimization only targeted at the constrained resource. This chapter contains 16 measurements and three reports that will contribute to the proper monitoring of a company that uses constraint management as its guiding principle. It also contains a discussion of those traditional measurements that will most negatively impact a constraint-based system, and which should therefore be avoided.

RATIO OF THROUGHPUT TO CONSTRAINT TIME CONSUMPTION

Product pricing should not be based on the underlying fully-absorbed cost of the product, but rather on the highest price that the market will tolerate. This concept will vary somewhat by company, depending on the presence of strategies to be the lowest-price competitor in the market, and the existing level of price competition. However, the key point is to *not* establish prices based on product cost.

The ratio of throughput to constraint time consumption is a good way to determine whether a product's price should be increased. If a product has a low throughput in proportion to the amount of constraint time used, the company should consider giving it a price increase in order to increase its net profits. Conversely, there should be an aggressive sales effort behind any product with a high throughput to constraint time consumption ratio, since this will lead to the highest possible profits. Finally, if a product uses no constraint time at all, then it can be priced just low enough to increase sales sufficiently to absorb any excess production capacity elsewhere in the production facility than in the constrained resource.

For example, the Professional Podcast Supply Company (PPS) has six products, as shown in the following table. It resells two products (headphones and a microphone), so neither one requires any constraint time. The remaining four products all require the use of a circuit board, which gives them all similar costs and identical throughput time in the circuit board assembly operation.

Product Name	Price	Variable Costs	Throughput	Constraint Time (min.)	Throughput to Constraint Time
Compressor	$219.00	$ 81.00	$138.00	14	$ 9.86/minute
Headphones	50.00	40.00	10.00	0	N/A
Microphone	300.00	240.00	60.00	0	N/A
Mixer	82.00	21.00	61.00	14	4.36/minute
Preamplifier	190.00	35.00	155.00	14	11.07/minute
Reverb board	140.00	28.00	112.00	14	8.00/minute

Based on the analysis in the table, PPS should attempt to increase the price of its mixer, which has a low throughput to constraint time ratio of $4.36 per minute, while boosting the sales effort for its preamplifier product, which has a ratio nearly three times higher. It should also consider dropping the prices of its headphone and microphone products to boost their unit sales, as long as the increased sales volume results in a net increase in total margins.

TOTAL THROUGHPUT DOLLARS QUOTED IN THE PERIOD

One of the measurements by which the sales department is usually judged is the total amount of sales dollars that it has quoted in a given period. The problem with this measurement is that it gives management no idea if the quoted sales contain a sufficient amount of throughput to ensure that the company will eventually earn a profit (subject, of course, to how many quotes are eventually converted into actual sales).

A better approach is to abandon the measurement of total quoted sales and replace it with total quoted throughput. This approach also provides management with a better tool for determining the proper sales compensation program, since it can configure commission levels to more highly compensate the sales staff if they quote high-throughput products and services. Otherwise, the sales staff will probably push products that they can most easily sell, irrespective of the level of throughput involved.

For example, the president of the Orion Telescope Company examines the results of the company's quoting activity for the most recent period, which is based on a flat-rate commission structure whereby the sales staff earns the same commission on all types of sales:

Product Name	Throughput/Unit	Units Quoted	Total Throughput	Commission Rate
8" Reflector	$ 220	800	$176,000	6%
4" Refractor	400	140	56,000	6%
12" Catadioptric	1,600	60	96,000	6%
	Totals	1,000	$328,000	

The sales staff claims that most customers want to purchase the 8-inch reflector telescope, because it has the lowest price. If so, Orion's throughput will remain low, since most sales quotes are focused on this low-throughput product. The president elects to test the sales staff's assertion by doubling the commission on the other two products, with the results shown in the following table:

Product Name	Throughput/Unit	Units Quoted	Total Throughput	Commission Rate
8″ Reflector	$ 220	700	$154,000	6%
4″ Refractor	400	180	72,000	12%
12″ Catadioptric	1,600	120	192,000	12%
	Totals	1,000	$418,000	

The table reveals that, though the total number of units quoted is identical to that of the previous month, the sales staff has convinced 10 percent of prospective customers to shift to higher-throughput products, with a resultant jump in the total quoted throughput of more than 27 percent over the preceding month.

RATIO OF THROUGHPUT DOLLARS QUOTED TO THROUGHPUT FIRM ORDERS RECEIVED

A prime measure of the sales department's effectiveness is to compare the total throughput dollars it has quoted to total throughput dollars received in firm orders. This shows its ability to convince a customer to accept a quote. A variation on this measurement is to calculate it only for those quotes for which there were competing quotes; this gives management a better idea of how well the company's offerings and price points compare to those of competing companies.

For example, the sales manager of the Air Spy Company, which conducts aerial surveys for municipal governments, creates the following table showing its ratio for sole source and competitive bid situations:

Quote Type	Throughput Quoted	Throughput Orders	Success Rate
Sole source	$ 4,825,000	$3,957,000	82%
Competitive bid	7,043,000	1,620,000	23%
Totals	$11,868,000	$5,577,000	47%

The table shows a common situation, where the effectiveness of the sales department will be maximized when it bids on sole source aerial photography projects.

SALES PRODUCTIVITY

The best way to measure the sales department's efficiency is to compare the total throughput dollars it has booked in each period to the department's expense. This shows how well the department's employees can uncover sales prospects and convert them into firm orders with the minimum amount of operating expense. The measurement is as follows:

$$\frac{\text{Throughput dollars booked}}{\text{Sales department expense}}$$

This measurement is particularly useful for judging the efficiency of sales that require a considerable amount of sales effort, such as those requiring product or service customization, multiple quote iterations, or extensive salesperson travel. For sales of this type, it is not uncommon to find that the sales productivity level is extremely low, possibly leading to the conclusion that other types of product sales will yield a higher level of sales productivity. However, this measurement does not reflect the impact of a long sales cycle, since there may be many months of apparently unproductive sales effort leading up to one very large order. It can also be distorted by the introduction of new products, which may cause sales to suddenly rise without much additional sales cost.

For example, the controller of the Cafeteria Carts company, maker of food catering carts, is becoming concerned that the sales staff is spending a great deal of its time assisting customers with the design of highly customized food carts, rather than selling its mass-produced carts. She creates the following table to reveal the sales productivity level for each type of cart sale:

Sale Type	Throughput Dollars Booked	Sales Department Expense	Sales Productivity
Custom carts	$ 5,750,000	$2,300,000	2.5
Standard carts	8,425,000	575,000	14.7
Totals	$14,175,000	$2,875,000	4.9

The table reveals a huge difference in sales productivity between the two types of sales. The sales department brings in only $2\frac{1}{2}$ times its costs when it sells customized carts, as opposed to almost 15 times its costs when it sells standardized carts.

RATIO OF THROUGHPUT BOOKED TO SHIPPED

The management team needs to know how many throughput dollars have been booked in each period. When tracked on a trend line in comparison to the dollars of throughput shipped each month, one can see if the company is altering the net amount of its backlogged throughput. This information can be used to alter the amount of resources assigned to the sales department or the constrained resource.

For example, the general manager of the American Playground Company (maker of durable playground equipment) has tracked in the following table the status of new throughput bookings, throughput shipped, and the net change between the two for the past six months:

Month	New Throughput Booked	Throughput Shipped	Net Throughput Change
January	$3,247,000	$3,107,000	$140,000
February	3,248,000	3,100,000	148,000
March	3,250,000	3,093,000	157,000
April	3,251,000	3,088,000	163,000
May	3,254,000	3,083,000	171,000
June	3,258,000	3,078,000	180,000

The table reveals that American Playground has a serious resource constraint problem, because its bookings are consistently exceeding its ability to ship, resulting in a continually expanding backlog and presumably longer period of time to fill orders. Furthermore, the difference between bookings and shipments is gradually expanding over time as its shipments decline, so the company appears to have a worsening problem.

TREND LINE OF SALES BACKLOG DOLLARS

When a company first identifies its constrained resource and begins work on improving the efficiency of that operation, it can be difficult finding an appropriate way to measure its success. One of the simplest measures is to track the total amount of sales backlog dollars on a trend line. If the backlog steadily declines, this indicates that the company is succeeding in breaking the constraint.

However, this measurement can also be misleading. A declining sales backlog may also be the result of a less efficient sales effort, old products that are being superseded in the marketplace, or excessively high product price points. Thus, it should always be combined with a measure of total sales achieved for the period to ensure that the backlog decline is not simply being caused by a decline in booked sales. An alternative measurement is the trend line of the ratio of throughput booked to shipped, as shown in the preceding measurement.

RATIO OF MAINTENANCE DOWNTIME TO OPERATING TIME ON CONSTRAINED RESOURCE

The maintenance staff should be measured based on its ability to keep the constrained resource running for long periods of time. This means that the effectiveness of its maintenance is more important than its efficiency in conducting a repair. In other words, the maintenance staff should be considered less successful if it spends just a few minutes correcting a problem that only keeps the constrained resource running for a short period of time; conversely, it is better to spend more time on a maintenance operation if this will result in a substantially longer operating period before the next machine stoppage for additional maintenance.

The best measurement for tracking this issue of maintenance effectiveness over efficiency is to compare the total time required for maintenance to the total machine downtime for the constrained resource. If the constrained resource is only run for one or two shifts out of the day, then only the maintenance time conducted during this operating period should be included in the numerator; this is an important concept, for the maintenance staff should always work outside of normal business hours on the constrained resource if this will contribute to a greater level of throughput. The measurement is:

$$\frac{\text{Total downtime for maintenance}}{\text{Total operating time of constrained resource}}$$

For example, the Klaus Candy Company produces a signature line of hard candies in the shape of various Christmas-related figures. Its constrained resource is the bagging operation, which mixes the various hard candies on a vibrating metal tray and seals them into a standard eight-ounce bag. The bagging operation runs for two shifts per day (960 minutes), and has a daily output of 28,800 bags, or 30 bags per minute. Each bag has throughput of $1.20, so the operation can potentially produce $34,560 per day of throughput, or $36.00 per minute. The maintenance staff conducts one hour of downtime per day to adjust the machine, as well as an additional 20 minutes to correct more critical issues, which reduces total operating time to 880 minutes (960 available minutes minus 80 maintenance minutes). This is a ratio of maintenance downtime to operating time of:

$$\frac{80 \text{ maintenance minutes}}{880 \text{ operating minutes}} = 9\%$$

This level of maintenance also represents a throughput loss of $2,880 per day ($36.00 throughput per minute × 80 maintenance minutes). The maintenance manager decides to pay overtime to his staff in order to shift the one hour of routine adjustment maintenance into the third shift, when the bagging machine is not operating. This increases throughput by $2,160 ($36.00 throughput per minute × 60 maintenance minutes) and also shrinks the ratio of maintenance downtime to operating time to 2.1 percent (20 maintenance minutes divided by 940 operating minutes).

THROUGHPUT OF POST-CONSTRAINT SCRAP

An excellent way to increase the total amount of system throughput is to avoid scrap that occurs after the constraint. These items have already been processed by the constrained resource, and so have used up bottleneck capacity that cannot be recovered. Consequently, one of the best throughput-related measurements is for scrap occurring after the constrained resource. The measurement is to compile the constraint hours spent to produce all scrap occurring after the constraint, and then multiply this by the average throughput per hour generated by the constraint. The calculation follows:

(Constraint hours spent to produce scrap) × (Throughput per hour)

Conversely, scrap occurring before the constrained resource does not impact constraint utilization, and so is much less important from the perspective of throughput generation.

For example, the primary component of the Dumper Wheelbarrow Company's legendary HaulMax Wheelbarrow is its oversized, heavy-gauge steel tray. The company's constrained resource is a sheet metal bending machine required to produce each tray. Subsequently, holes are drilled in the tray so that it can be bolted to the wheelbarrow frame. If the holes are drilled off-center, then the wheelbarrow must be scrapped.

A number of trays are being scrapped because of this drilling problem. Dumper's controller wants to determine the cost of post-constraint scrap. To do so, she accumulates the number of scrapped trays in the past month (120 trays) and uses routing documents to determine the average amount of constraint time used for the production of each tray (0.15 hours). She then calculates the constraint's average throughput per hour as $1,850. With this information, she compiles the cost of post-constraint scrap as follows:

(120 scrapped trays × 0.15 hours) × ($1,850 throughput per hour)

= $33,300

Wooden frames for the HaulMax do not use the constrained resource at all, but are still subject to drilling problems that require many frames to be discarded. Dumper's controller calculates the cost of these scrapped items as the number of units scrapped (190 in the past month) multiplied by the variable cost of each frame ($17), which is a total cost of $3,230. Clearly, Dumper should concentrate its efforts on fixing the downstream tray drilling problem rather than the unrelated frame drilling problem in order to more quickly maximize its throughput.

CONSTRAINT UTILIZATION

The constrained resource should be operated at a very high level of efficiency in order to maximize system throughput. A good measure for this core operation is constraint utilization, which is the actual hours of constraint run time divided by the number of constraint hours available for use. The calculation is:

$$\frac{\text{Actual production hours of constraint operation}}{\text{Constraint hours available}}$$

The constraint utilization measure can be manipulated by running low-priority jobs through the work center, just to keep the machine running. If this appears to be a problem, consider also measuring the constrained resource using the constraint schedule attainment measurement (discussed in the next section), which verifies that the correct jobs are being run through the constrained resource. Also, the denominator can be artificially reduced in order to increase the apparent level of utilization. It is generally best to assume that there are 24 constraint hours available per day, and not allow anyone to reduce this figure. The constraint utilization and constraint schedule attainment measures are the best two ways to judge the performance of the constraint manager. A supplemental measure for performance measurement could be some determination of the reduction in job setup times on the constraint, since this impacts total throughput.

For example, the Blowhard Glass Works has determined that its annealer furnace, which is used to slowly cool shaped glass to room temperature, is its constrained resource. The furnace is usually operational 24 hours a day on a perpetual basis, so constraint utilization is always 100 percent. In this instance, the proper measurement is to track the proportion of the annealer that is filled during the cool-down process, since Blowhard can achieve a higher level of throughput if the annealer is fully loaded at all times. In the past month, the annealer was only 48 percent filled on average, so this is the most acceptable utilization measurement to use.

CONSTRAINT SCHEDULE ATTAINMENT

As noted in the description for the preceding constraint utilization measurement, it is possible for the manager of the constrained resource to artificially show strong utilization performance by running low-priority jobs through the constraint. To guard against this, use the constraint schedule attainment measurement to verify that the correct jobs are being run through the constraint. The measurement is to divide the number of scheduled jobs completed by the number of scheduled jobs. It is important to keep the measurement period relatively short, such as a week, so that the constraint manager cannot run a job scheduled for late in the measurement period in advance of jobs scheduled earlier. If this happens, the measurement may show a high level of performance while selected shipments are actually late. The calculation follows:

$$\frac{\text{Number of scheduled jobs completed}}{\text{Number of scheduled jobs in the measurement period}}$$

This measurement is most effective when there are many short-duration jobs being run through the constraint, because it yields a more accurate measurement. At the opposite extreme, if only a single job is being run through the constraint during the entire measurement period, the result will be 0 percent performance, since no scheduled jobs were completed.

As an example, the SafeFlight Corporation produces the Bi-Push Commuter, which is a small rear-propeller plane with a carbon composite body, designed for low-cost, short-duration commuter flights. SafeFlight has a backlog of 550 Bi-Push planes, and it is having difficulty meeting its production schedule because of its constrained resource, which is the composites lamination department. Bubbles are appearing at random in the lamination, requiring the scrapping or rework of some body components. The constraint schedule attainment measurement covers a one-month period. The following table shows measurement results for the past four months:

Month	Scheduled Production Units	Completed Production Units	Constraint Schedule Attainment
January	18	17	94%
February	20	16	80%
March	22	15	68%
April	24	14	58%

The table clearly shows that SafeFlight has not yet worked through the production problems facing its composites lamination department, and in fact is increasing its production schedule each month under the false assumption that the constraint is improving its efficiency, when the opposite is occurring. In this case, a poor constraint schedule attainment measurement may not be entirely the fault of the constraint manager, but rather of the industrial engineers who have clearly not fixed the underlying production flaws.

MANUFACTURING PRODUCTIVITY

Though throughput accounting clearly places the greatest emphasis on increasing system throughput, it is still important to keep costs in perspective. To do this, compare throughput dollars to operating expenses, which yields the productivity of the manufacturing operation. To measure it, divide total throughput dollars shipped during the period to total production expenses incurred. The calculation follows:

$$\frac{\text{Throughput dollars shipped}}{\text{Production expenses incurred}}$$

Alternatively, change the denominator to be *all* company expenses incurred, which gives a better picture of how every expenditure, anywhere in the company, impacts throughput. This broader perspective is especially useful when sales are strongly driven by a large and expensive sales force.

Manufacturing productivity can be used to show how reductions in operating expenses impact throughput. For example, if the production manager feels that headcount can be reduced without impacting throughput, then try it for a few months and see what happens to the ratio. However, it is best to test the impact of such changes over multiple months, since reductions in operating expenses frequently reduce the amount of sprint capacity available in the production process, which will only become evident at long intervals, when rare but large upstream production variations cause the constrained resource to run out of work.

This measurement can also be used to determine the impact of increases in operating expenses on throughput, which can occur if the incremental cost increases will support more throughput at the constrained resource.

Finally, if there are shipment problems, this will be revealed as a worsening productivity ratio, since throughput will decline.

For example, the Bingo Bakery wants to lower its operating expenses by using heat transfer pumps to shift heat from its baking ovens to its low temperature proofing ovens, which are used to trigger the yeast in the bread prior to final baking. The cost of the heat transfer pumps is $190,000, which is offset by annual reductions of $100,000 in the amount of natural gas needed to fire the heaters under the proofing ovens. There is no impact on throughput. Bingo current has annual throughput of $10.5 million and operating expenses of $7.2 million, which is a manufacturing productivity ratio of 146 percent ($10.5 million throughput/$7.2 million operating expenses). After the heat transfer pumps are installed, the productivity ratio improves to 148 percent ($10.5 million throughput/$7.1 million operating expenses).

MANUFACTURING EFFECTIVENESS

The manufacturing process should also be judged based on the amount of throughput achieved for every hour of constraint time used. If the manufacturing staff can reduce rework and scrap levels occurring after the constrained resource, or improve the processing speed of the constraint, or shorten the duration of job setups on the constraint, then it can increase the amount of throughput dollars shipped for every hour of constraint time used. The measurement is to divide total throughput dollars shipped during the measurement period by the number of hours during which the constrained resource was in use. The calculation follows:

$$\frac{\text{Throughput dollars shipped}}{\text{Constraint hours used}}$$

However, this measurement is also strongly impacted by the mix of products sold by the company, as well as by the scheduling of those customer orders through the constrained resource. If the sales department runs a price discount on a low-throughput product and is swamped by orders, then the manufacturing manager will suffer with a low manufacturing effectiveness ratio due to the reduced through-put dollars in the calculation's numerator. Similarly, if the materials manager schedules the production of low-throughput products because he does not have some raw materials available for high-throughput products, then again the manufacturing effectiveness ratio will suffer.

ORDER CYCLE TIME

The faster a company can process orders through its entire production system, the faster it can realize more throughput and therefore more profit. Though the volume of orders processed is entirely driven by the capacity of the constrained resource, other parts of the production process can be compressed to achieve a shorter total order cycle time. Having a demonstrably shorter cycle time than competitors may result in more orders, though this will only create a larger backlog in front of the constraint resource (unless it is supplemented with other capacity, such as additional labor, machinery, or outsourcing). The order cycle time calculation is to subtract the order receipt date from the ship date for each shipped order, and create an average for all such orders. The calculation follows:

(Ship date) − (Date of receipt of order)

This measurement tends to result in artificially low order cycle times, because the person conducting the calculation only includes orders that have actually shipped. However, there are usually a few orders that are massively delayed for various reasons, and for which there is no ship date. Be sure to include these orders in the measurement, using the calculation date as the ship date—the result may be a dramatic lengthening of the average order cycle time.

For example, the Marine Granite Company, purveyors of fine marble tiling for oceangoing yachts, must process orders on a timely basis or incur the wrath of its wealthy clients. Some types of granite must be flown in from remote areas of Italy, and so can be delayed well beyond the norm. Its order cycle information for the past month is as follows:

Order Number	Ship Date	Order Date	Cycle Time (days)
200603	None	January 11	139
200641	None	February 6	114
200832	May 17	April 23	24
200833	May 19	April 26	23
200834	May 25	April 30	26
200835	May 25	May 3	22
200836	May 26	May 9	17
200837	May 29	May 9	20
200838	May 31	May 12	19

If Marine Granite's cycle time calculation is only based on the final seven orders on the list (which are the ones for which shipment has been completed), then the average cycle time appears to be a reasonable 21.6 days. However, this would not include the two orders for which granite has not yet been received from Italy; if these are included (assuming a May 31 measurement date), then the average cycle time increases substantially, to 44.9 days.

THROUGHPUT SHIPPING DELAY

Though the constrained resource is the primary determinant of the amount of throughput that can be shipped, there can also be delays later in the production process that keep orders from being shipped. Thus, throughput dollars shipped may be substantially less than the throughput dollars processed by the constraint. To see if this problem exists, it is useful to track the throughput shipping delay. The calculation is to divide the amount of throughput dollars shipped late (or not yet shipped at all) by the total throughput scheduled for shipment during the period.

$$\frac{\text{Throughput dollars scheduled for shipment in the period but not shipped}}{\text{Throughput dollars scheduled for shipment in the period}}$$

This measurement is designed to support the customer service function, since it reveals the proportion of orders shipped late (even if the delay is only a single day). A variation on this measurement is to only include in the denominator the throughput dollars scheduled for shipment that were not shipped *at all* during the reporting period—this measurement is more useful from the accounting perspective, since it reveals the reduction of profits that is directly attributable to late shipments.

For example, the Big Round Tire Company sends custom drag racing tires to clients around the world by air express. Timely delivery is extremely important. Big Round creates its own tires, and has been having trouble processing sufficient quantities of green (uncured) tires through its curing station to meet scheduled shipment dates. In the most recent month, shipments representing 22 percent of all throughput dollars were shipped after their scheduled shipment dates. Further, one-third of the orders in the 22 percent measurement were not shipped as of month-end, resulting in a throughput shortfall for the month of $231,000. The 22 percent throughput shipping delay is used to measure the company's customer service performance, while the $231,000 of lost throughput is used to explain a portion of Big Round's loss for the month.

INVENTORY TURNOVER

Inventory turnover is traditionally defined to be the annualized cost of goods sold divided by the average level of on-hand inventory. Both the values in the numerator and denominator usually include fully burdened costs. In particular, the cost of goods sold in the numerator can be quite large, since a wide array of overhead costs may be added to it. The result tends to be a relatively low inventory turnover figure, which management is constantly striving to reduce on the grounds that excessive inventory balances tie up too much invested capital.

In a throughput environment, the inventory turnover calculation changes, as does the application of overhead costs to the both components of the calculation. Further, it is used in a different manner to manage the business.

When measuring inventory turnover with a goal of maximizing the use of a constrained resource, the key issue is how much inventory is needed to maximize throughput. With this goal in mind, the cost of goods sold is replaced in the numerator by throughput dollars. Inventory remains in the denominator, but the amount shown is strictly the variable cost of the inventory. Overhead is not added to any part of this calculation. The calculation follows:

$$\frac{\text{Annual throughput}}{\text{Acquisition cost of on-hand inventory}}$$

By using this approach, management can now determine the incremental investment in inventory that it should (or should not) make in order to achieve the highest possible level of throughput. Adding overhead to either side of the calculation merely muddies the result, since overhead is comprised of operating expenses, which will not vary incrementally with changes in throughput or inventory. This measurement no longer automatically results in a management decision to reduce inventory levels. Instead, the more common result is to avoid reducing any inventory that will impact throughput (e.g., the inventory buffer in front of the constrained resource), though inventory levels elsewhere in the system may decline.

For example, the J-Stroke Company builds a traditional strip-built birch bark canoe. Strips are taken from birch planks to construct each canoe in a series of lamination steps. The problem is that many birch planks contain flaws in the grain which are only discovered during the production process, so a great deal of raw material must be stocked to ensure that sufficient inventory is available to keep production running smoothly. J-Stroke's current inventory investment is $620,000, and its annual throughput is $4,250,000, which represents inventory turnover of 6.9 ($4,250,000 annual throughput/$620,000 inventory). If J-Stroke invests in an additional $100,000 of birch planks, it estimates that its constraint resource will suffer less downtime, resulting in increased throughput of $210,000. The resulting inventory turnover would be 6.2 ($4,460,000 annual throughput/$720,000 inventory). Thus, an *increase* in inventory also increases throughput, which is a desirable outcome, despite the resulting decline in inventory turnover.

RETURN ON INVESTMENT

In throughput accounting, there are few investments made, with the exception of inventory. The general assumption is that the system already has an excess level of capacity (with the exception of the constrained resource), so capital investments are not common. Inventory levels, however, may change with some frequency as management tries to determine the optimum mix of inventory needed to support the highest possible level of throughput. For these reasons, the return on investment calculation most commonly used in throughput accounting is net profit divided by the acquisition cost of on-hand inventory. The calculation follows:

$$\frac{\text{Net profit}}{\text{Acquisition cost of on-hand inventory}}$$

For example, the Ashley Spinning Wheel Company wants to increase sales of its signature birch home spinning wheel by stocking more finished goods for its primary summer sales season. Historically, if Ashley runs out of finished goods during this time period, potential customers will buy from competitors rather than Ashley. In this case, the constraint is in the market, not Ashley's production facility, so it can increase production levels. Ashley's sales manager estimates that an additional 240 spinning wheels should be held in stock for the summer sales season. The materials cost of each spinning wheel is $315, which represents a total investment of $75,600. No additional overhead or labor costs are added to this investment amount, since those costs are charged off as operating expenses as incurred. Ashley then realizes sales of 195 spinning wheels as a result of this new inventory stocking policy. Each spinning wheel sells for $750. Its return on investment calculation follows:

$$\frac{(\$750 \text{ price} - \$315 \text{ materials cost}) \times 195 \text{ units sold}}{\$315 \text{ materials cost} \times 240 \text{ units held in inventory}}$$

$$= 12.2\% \text{ return on investment}$$

THROUGHPUT CONTRIBUTION REPORT

Though most accountants know the fully burdened cost of their company's products, we have shown in this book that fully burdened

Product Name	Price	Variable Cost	Throughput	Constraint Time Used (minutes)	Throughput Time per Unit
42″ Plasma TV	$3,100	$2,020	$1,080	20	$54.00
24″ CRT Monitor	800	520	280	6	46.67
13″ B&W TV	120	70	50	2	25.00
30″ LCD TV	1,200	575	625	40	15.63
19″ LCD Monitor	290	230	60	14	4.29

EXHIBIT 8.1 THROUGHPUT CONTRIBUTION REPORT

costs are irrelevant in throughput accounting. Instead, replace fully burdened cost reports with a throughput contribution report, such as the one shown in Exhibit 8.1. This report focuses on only two items of information—the throughput generated by each product and the time required to process it at the constrained resource. By then dividing constraint time used into throughput, we arrive at throughput time per unit. Thus, the throughput contribution report reveals the amount of throughput generated for the least amount of constraint usage. This information can then be used to determine the best mix of products to sell in order to maximize throughput.

As shown in Exhibit 8.1, the throughput contribution report can be sorted in declining order by throughput time per unit, so the products yielding the best return on constrain usage are listed at the top. In this case, the 42-inch plasma television yields the best throughput per minute of constraint usage, at $54.00 per minute.

BUFFER MANAGEMENT REPORT

There is a strong need for an inventory buffer in front of the constrained resource, so that variations in upstream production activities do not result in a work stoppage on the constraint. The buffer management report shown in Exhibit 8.2 is designed to give details about problems that caused shrinkage in the size of the buffer (buffer penetration). Management uses it to track down and correct buffer-related problems.

Since the buffer management report is designed to spot problems upstream from the buffer, it can also be used to evaluate the performance of whomever manages those upstream operations.

Date	Arrival Time Required	Actual Arrival Time	Originating Work Station	Cause of Delay
Sept. 11	9/11, 2 P.M.	9/12, 3 P.M.	Paint shop	Paint nozzles clogged
Sept. 14	9/14, 9 A.M.	9/16, 4 P.M.	Electrolysis	Power outage
Sept. 19	9/19, 10 A.M.	9/19, 4 P.M.	Electrolysis	Electrodes corroded
Sept. 19	9/19, 4 P.M.	9/25, 10 A.M.	Paint shop	Paint nozzles clogged
Sept. 23	9/23, 1 P.M.	9/24, 9 A.M.	Paint shop	Ran out of paint

EXHIBIT 8.2 BUFFER MANAGEMENT REPORT

BUFFER HOLE PERCENTAGE TREND REPORT

Management needs a tool for determining the correct size of any inventory buffers used. Though it can initially be set based on a rough estimate, ongoing monitoring of buffer penetrations is needed to decide if the buffer should be increased or reduced in size.

The proper tool for buffer size management is the buffer hole percentage trend report, as shown in Exhibit 8.3. The report shows an upper and lower boundary line, which represent tolerable boundaries for the percentage of all jobs where shipments caused the expedite portion of the buffer to be penetrated. The expedite zone is that portion of the buffer where a lack of inventory from an upstream work center will trigger expediting to ensure that replenishment inventory arrives

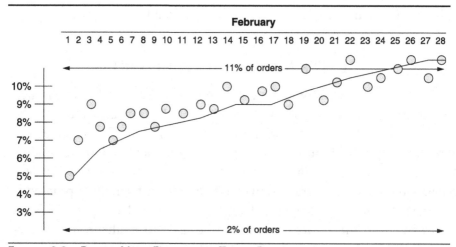

EXHIBIT 8.3 BUFFER HOLE PERCENTAGE TREND REPORT

as soon as possible. The small circles represent the daily percentage of jobs causing buffer penetration, while the line running approximately through the center of the boundary limits is a multi-day moving average of the percentage of expedited orders experienced.

An in-condition situation is when the moving-average line stays within the upper and lower boundaries. If it regularly strays outside the top boundary, then the buffer should be increased in size to reduce the risk of total buffer penetration; if it stays outside the lower boundary, then the buffer is too large and should be reduced. In the exhibit, the trend line has repeatedly exceeded the top boundary, so it appears that a larger buffer is needed.

MISLEADING MEASUREMENTS AND REPORTS

Many traditional measurements and reports are not useful in constraint management, because they are strongly focused on local optimization, which does not improve total profits. Here are some of the more common measurements and reports to avoid, and why:

- *Sales per person.* Sales do not lead to profitability unless the sales have a sufficiently high level of throughput. Also, this measure tends to lead to overall headcount reductions in order to improve the ratio, when in fact staffing is needed not only at the constrained resource, but also wherever sprint capacity is needed in upstream workstations.
- *Overhead percentage.* This is total overhead expense divided by direct labor. Since operating expenses are charged off in the current period, there should be no overhead to allocate. Also, since there is no clear relationship between direct labor and overhead expenses, it would be useless to allocate overhead (even if it existed in a throughput environment, which it does not) using direct labor.
- *Labor cost component.* This measurement itemizes the standard or actual cost of labor consumed by each unit produced. The problem is that management uses it to focus on eliminating labor costs, usually by installing automated equipment. When the automated equipment is used, there is a tendency to justify

its purchase by running it at a high utilization level, resulting in an excessive amount of work-in-process inventory on hand.

- *Break-even point.* This is the point at which the sale of average fully-burdened products results in sufficient gross margins to break even. The trouble is that the gross margins used in the calculations include a large amount of overhead costs, resulting in margins that are far too low. The measurement should instead replace the gross margin with the average throughput percentage, and add direct labor and overhead costs to the operating expenses in the numerator.

- *Gross profit percentage.* This is the most common tool used to evaluate the profitability of products. However, since each one is assigned an overhead cost in addition to the totally variable expenses normally used in throughput accounting, the gross profit percentage is always too low. This can result in the termination of products that actually had some positive throughput, and which therefore should have been retained.

- *Working capital.* A major component of working capital is inventory. However, the recorded inventory cost includes a large overhead cost component, which under throughput accounting is charged off in the current period as an operating expense. Thus, the traditional working capital measure is too high by the amount of overhead contained in the inventory figure.

- *Economic production run size.* This measurement is used to determine the optimum number of units to run through a production work center as a single batch, with a major determinant being the job setup duration. However, excessively large batch sizes can result in a shortage of inventory in front of the constrained resource, so using the measurement can result in a throughput reduction.

- *Work-in-process turnover.* This measurement compares the cost of goods sold to the amount of inventory located in the work-in-process (WIP) area, with the usual result being an ongoing drive to reduce WIP inventory. However, it is mandatory to position a buffer in front of the constrained resource, so shrinking WIP indiscriminately can result in serious throughput reductions.

- *Return on assets.* This measurement compares net income to a company's total asset base. However, many assets are superfluous in a constraint management environment, or merely represent a vastly excessive level of capacity. The result is a return on assets that is far lower than the return on key assets employed in the production process.
- *Machine efficiency report.* This report itemizes the proportion of available time that each machine was used, throughout the production facility. This is one of the worst possible reports for management to rely on, since there is a natural tendency to maximize machine usage everywhere in the facility, which results in far too much work-in-process inventory.
- *Overtime report.* This report shows the overtime hours and related cost worked by all hourly employees. Management uses this report to coordinate workloads in order to reduce overtime costs. However, doing so may take staff away from the constrained resource, which may require overtime work to maximize its utilization.
- *Scrap report.* This report shows the various types and quantities of scrap incurred everywhere in the production facility, as well as the fully burdened cost of the scrap. Though the intent is good, the report does not differentiate between scrap occurring before and after the constrained resource. Also, scrap costs incurred before the constraint should be reported at their variable costs only, while costs incurred after the constraint should be reported at the average throughput rate for the facility.

SUMMARY

This chapter showed that an entirely new set of measurements must be used to monitor the results of a system whose primary goal is to maximize the use of a constrained resource in order to maximize throughput. In many cases, traditional measurements and reports are not only misleading, but exceptionally counterproductive to the achievement of this goal. Thus, when designing a measurement and reporting system that supports throughput concepts, it is best to completely eliminate from consideration the entire existing structure of measurements and reports in favor of the new systems outlined in this chapter. Traditional measurements should only be used after considerable review of their potential impact on constraint and throughput management.

9

THROUGHPUT AND ACCOUNTING MANAGEMENT

The beauty of constraint management is that it focuses attention on just a small number of weak links in the production system. This makes it much easier to determine the exact amount of system improvement gained by improving the performance of these few weak links. Thus, an improvement in the efficiency of the constrained resource, or an increase in the inventory buffer, or of sprint capacity, will have an almost immediate impact on throughput that can be measured with some accuracy. Consider the alternative, which is the traditional method of spraying improvements all over the factory and hoping that they will somehow result in increased profits. This chapter contains a number of decision areas on which the accounting manager should focus in order to maximize a company's use of constraint management. For easy reference, the decision areas addressed in this chapter are as follows:

1. Throughput analysis priorities
2. The subordination concept
3. The duration of capacity constraints
4. The inventory build concept
5. The capacity–buffer interrelationship
6. Investment analysis
7. Price formulation
8. Transfer pricing
9. Cost reporting
10. Staffing decisions

11.   The problem with using throughput accounting for tactical changes
12.   Throughput software and makeshift systems

THROUGHPUT ANALYSIS PRIORITIES

Throughput analysis includes the calculation of an action's impact on throughput, invested funds, and operating expenses. When conducting an analysis and making a recommendation based on throughput concepts, how should the accountant rank these three items?

An action that results in an increase in throughput should always be recommended to management more highly than one that reduces the level of investment or operating expenses. There are two reasons for this prioritization. First, there is no limit to increases in throughput, whereas the amount by which invested funds or operating expenses can be reduced has a downward limit. Second, reductions in investment or operating expenses tend to reduce the production capacity of the system, which in turn reduces throughput.

This does not mean that invested funds and operating expenses are *not* to be reduced, only that their impact on system capacity should be closely examined before being approved.

With throughput being the clear favorite for recommendation priorities, how should actions be prioritized that only impact invested funds or operating expenses? Generally, it is better to first recommend actions that reduce invested funds. The reason is that investment reduction is frequently coupled with inventory reduction. With the exception of inventory reductions in the constraint and final assembly buffers, throughput is actually *improved* through inventory reduction, because lower inventories reduce production lead time, rapidly reveal quality problems that can be quickly remedied, and therefore increase throughput.

It is also useful to review throughput analysis decisions based on a standard set of questions to see how proposed actions will result in changes to either throughput, invested funds, or operating expenses. For example, positive answers to the following questions will result in increases to throughput, and should probably be recommended, based on the extent of any offsetting impact on invested funds or operating expenses:

- Will the action increase total sales?
- Will the action result in better use of the constrained resource?
- Will the action shorten delivery times to customers?
- Will the action improve the product or service being provided?
- Will the action win repeat business?
- Will the action reduce scrap or rework?

Positive answers to the following questions will result in reductions in the level of invested funds, and so should be recommended, based on the extent of any offsetting impact on throughput or operating expenses:

- Will the company require fewer raw materials?
- Will the company reduce the amount of on-hand work-in-process inventory?
- Will the company require less on-hand finished goods inventory?
- Will the company require fewer capital assets to create products?

Similarly, positive answers to the following questions should result in approval to take the recommended action, subject to the extent of any offsetting impact on throughput or invested funds:

- Will the action reduce warranty costs?
- Will operating expenses decline?
- Will payments to suppliers decrease or be delayed?

In summary, most proposed actions resulting in increased throughput should be recommended, because long-term growth comes from improving the flow of materials through productive processes, rather than through piecemeal cost or investment reduction efforts.

THE SUBORDINATION CONCEPT

The accountant must be aware of the exact location of the constrained resource at all times, because many of a company's activities must then be subordinated to the maximization of that resource. Since the accountant is responsible for calculating and reporting the metrics issued to management, it is mandatory to suggest changes to the metrics if they will otherwise create incentives for employees to conduct activities that do not support the constraint. The same concept applies to policies and procedures that can impact the constraint.

For example, many companies issue bonuses to their employees if inventory levels can be driven as low as possible. By reducing inventory levels, a company reduces its work capital investment. However, there must always be a sufficiently large inventory buffer positioned in front of both the constrained resource and final assembly area, as described extensively in Chapter 2, Constraint Management in the Factory. Consequently, the inventory turnover metric can result in management actions to reduce the inventory buffer, which can result in the reduction of throughput. The accountant may need to alter the metric to not include work-in-process inventory (where the value of the constraint buffer is recorded) or to avoid reporting on the turnover figure altogether.

Another example of subordination problems is when the accountant reports on equipment utilization. This report typically shows utilization levels for work centers throughout the production facility, and leads managers to keep all of them operating at the highest possible levels of efficiency. The trouble is that only the constrained resource should operate at full capacity, with all other work centers operating at whatever usage level is needed to supply to constraint. Thus, a more appropriate reporting structure that leads to proper subordination is to only report on the utilization level of the constrained resource.

The accountant is also heavily involved in the analysis of investment requests for new capital items. The acquisition decision is usually heavily weighted in favor of the net present value calculated in a proposal. However, this can lead to investments that are not needed if they do not contribute to additional throughput. Thus, the accountant should modify the capital budgeting proposal and procedure, as noted in Chapter 5, Throughput in the Budgeting and Capital Budgeting Process, to ensure that capital expenditures are only made that increase the throughput of the constrained resource.

There are many more possible examples of the importance of subordination, but these examples are sufficient to show how the accountant must modify company systems to ensure that proper attention and resources are focused on the constrained resource.

THE DURATION OF CAPACITY CONSTRAINTS

A considerable proportion of this book has been devoted to the variety of ways to manage constrained resources within a company. However, once a company goes through a few rounds of improvements to how it supports its constraint (as alluded to in the last section), the company will usually have improved its throughput to such an extent that the constraint moves entirely out of the production area. Likely homes for the new constraint are the sales department (due to lack of sales staff) or the marketplace. The reason for this rapid shifting of the constraint out of the production area is that it was originally constructed with far too much production capacity. The company will then need to increase sales considerably before the constraint shifts back into the production area, quite possibly in a work center different from the original constraint location.

This concept has a major impact on accounting decisions, because the controller must be aware of the point at which the constraint shifts. When it does, the company should no longer invest in capacity improvements at the resource that was previously constrained, since any excess capacity there will no longer result in any increase in throughput. If the constraint shifts entirely out of the company and into the marketplace, then it may be necessary to plan for when increased demand in the future may call for new investments to keep capacity in line with that demand, and where the constraint may be at that time.

THE INVENTORY BUILD CONCEPT

This section addresses several scenarios under which inventory levels are increased, and how throughput analysis can be used to determine the efficacy of these decisions.

The accountant should be aware of changes in the level of all types of inventory, but especially of increases in finished goods, because it is a warning sign of several possible problems. One is that the constraint has been eliminated within the company, and has now shifted into the marketplace. If this is the case, then the company's production schedulers may be blithely continuing to maximize use of the former constraint's capacity, even though it is no longer needed, resulting in an increase in finished goods that cannot be sold. When this happens, the accountant must issue a warning to the management team about the new capacity situation, and work with them to revise production scheduling so that only enough units are produced to meet immediate demand.

Another possible problem is that production runs are being scheduled for more units than are actually needed for immediate sales. This is usually not a good scheduling choice, because the finished inventory being sent to the warehouse is using up time at the constraint that could have been used to meet immediate customer orders. The excessively long production runs are likely being driven by either the cost accountants or industrial engineers, who feel that excessively long setup times make it necessary to have long production runs in order to reduce the setup cost per unit. However, this is a false assumption in all areas outside of the constraint, since excess available capacity means that setups have no cost. Only in the case of the constrained resource itself can the use of extra-long production runs be validated, since an excessive amount of setup time in this area will take time away from the manufacture of products that can create immediate throughput. Thus, some balancing of setup duration against lost throughput can be a valid argument, but only at the constraint.

A third inventory build scenario is related to strong seasonal sales, such as the Christmas season. In this case, the system's production capacity is so far below the amount needed to meet a short spike in sales that inventory must be built for many months in advance. This is one of the few valid reasons for an inventory buildup, especially if management feels that it must employ some skilled manufacturing employees during all months of the year, irrespective of the level of demand.

A final inventory build decision involves the acquisition of an unusually large quantity of raw materials. This can be an excellent choice when the company anticipates that it will soon be put on materials allocation by a supplier, since the company is bolstering an anticipated capacity constraint. The same reasoning applies if a transport strike is anticipated, since the raw materials may be available at supplier locations, but there may be no means of transporting them to the company's production facility. In both cases, the decision to invest in more inventory is a good one, because of the anticipation that inventory will shortly become the constrained resource.

THE CAPACITY—BUFFER INTERRELATIONSHIP

The accounting manager is often asked to render an opinion on the need for more production capacity, usually through the review of a capital budgeting proposal. This review generally centers on the ability of the capital item to generate more cash flow than it costs. However, an analysis using throughput accounting will result in fewer capital assets, because it will show that only additions to the constrained resource will result in more throughput.

However, there is somewhat more to this analysis than a simple is-it-at-the-constraint-or-not decision. There is also a close interrelationship between the size of the inventory buffer and the need for more capacity. If there is a large amount of inventory positioned in front of the constrained resource, then there is more time available for upstream resources to catch up in the event of an unexpected upstream production stoppage. Thus, with more inventory on hand, there is less need for additional capacity. Conversely, if there is only a small inventory buffer on hand, there may be a considerable need for more capacity in order to ensure that the constraint is always supplied with a sufficient amount of input to stay operational at all times.

This is a useful concept when the sales department accepts a large amount of new orders, because it introduces the possibility of another option besides the acquisition of more capacity. In some cases where new upstream capacity is only needed to help rebuild the inventory buffer, the accountant can suggest the use of outsourcing to rebuild the buffer. Since this is a one-time use (e.g., buffer rebuild) rather than an ongoing capacity need, it may be more cost-effective to pay a higher price per unit in the short term to rebuild a buffer than it would to invest in expensive new equipment.

INVESTMENT ANALYSIS

The investment analysis task should follow the methodology outlined in Chapter 4, Throughput and Financial Analysis Scenarios, where an investment is acceptable if it results in a net increase in throughput without a large increase in operating expenses. However, there is also a more subtle investment scenario that the accountant should be aware of.

Most companies do not experience a sudden increase in product sales—rather, they are subject to a slow, steady increase in demand that gradually fills the available amount of capacity throughout the production area. When this happens, management attention is rightly focused on maintaining a high level of throughput at the constrained resource. However, the increased demand also tends to gradually absorb excess capacity levels elsewhere in the plant. If this phenomenon continues for some time, management may be blindsided by what appears to be a sudden decrease in sprint capacity.

If sprint capacity declines to an excessive extent, it is likely that occasional upstream production problems will eventually result in a severe buffer penetration from which the company cannot recover, resulting in shortages at the constraint and a reduction of throughput. To guard against the onset of this creeping reduction in capacity, the accountant should monitor non-constraint usage levels, and warn management when there is a long-term reduction of sprint capacity that is not abating. This may very well call for additional investments in order to maintain a sufficient level of sprint capacity.

The same concept can be applied to judging the timing of capacity additions at the constrained resource. If the constraint is subject to unusually large work queues that persist for a long period of time, the accountant should recommend an increase in the permanent capacity of the constraint. However, the measurement period should take into account the presence of any sales seasonality, in case the observed queue levels are merely associated with a normal seasonal increase that will subsequently decline.

PRICE FORMULATION

The accounting manager likely becomes involved in product price setting, if only for special one-time pricing situations. In these cases, the sales manager receives an offer to sell a large quantity at a low price, and the accounting manager is asked if a sufficient profit can be obtained from the deal. Rather than reiterate the multitude of analyses from Chapter 4 Throughput and Financial Analysis Scenarios, the main point is that the throughput analysis model is made extremely simple to use by avoiding cost allocations. The basic rule for throughput-based price setting is that, if a company is bidding on a sale and the product passes through the constrained resource, then the company should only bid if the product's throughput per minute at the constraint exceeds the throughput per minute of at least the lowest-throughput item currently being produced. Based on its ease of understandability and speed with which decisions can be made, the throughput model is clearly superior to the use of fully-allocated costing models to determine appropriate price points.

The setting of a proper price point becomes more judgmental if the constraint moves to the market. In this case, a company may be tempted to increase its sales by means of a price cut, which it has the capability to effect when there is no in-house constraint. However, a price cut is easily copied by competitors. A better approach is to create a more permanent basis of competition that other companies cannot readily match, one that could even involve a price *increase*. For example, there may be such an excessive level of capacity available that the company can accept the need for many setups that would accompany a new order policy allowing the placement of very small order sizes. Similarly, it could promise shorter intervals before orders are shipped. These are examples of changes that address core customer problems, and which are more likely to not only win new customers, but also retain them over the long term.

TRANSFER PRICING

Larger corporations frequently have different divisions that use each other's products as inputs into their own products, which may in turn be shifted to yet another division as input into their products. If company divisions are *required* to use other divisions as their suppliers, then throughput analysis does not enter into the decision to acquire materials. However, if they are allowed to choose *any* supplier, then consider using throughput analysis as part of the procurement decision.

The price imposed on a division to purchase a part from another corporate division may involve the decision to artificially raise or lower the price in order to recognize a correspondingly lower or higher profit, depending on the tax jurisdiction of the division. For example, if a division is located in a tax jurisdiction where tax rates are extremely low, then the corporate tax manager will likely recommend that the transfer price that division pays be unusually low, so that it can recognize a large profit and pay a relatively small tax on it. From the perspective of the accountant at the division level, throughput analysis shows that the totally variable cost of the incoming product is probably lower if bought from another corporate division than from an outside supplier, because of the artificially low transfer price.

However, the scenario may change when viewed from the perspective of the corporate tax manager. If this person has access to the cost of competing products from outside suppliers, it may become evident that the corporation as a whole would benefit more by increasing the artificial interdivision transfer price in order to allow the division to purchase elsewhere, if competing prices are extremely low. This analysis would essentially be a comparison of the reduction in actual variable cost to be achieved by using an outside supplier to the increased tax cost of shifting the recognition of income to the division residing in an area with the next lowest income tax rate. Unfortunately, tax managers rarely attempt to access such a detailed level of information, so most companies transacting business amongst their own divisions face the prospect of incurring suboptimal total profits.

However, having presented the use of throughput analysis for the transfer pricing decision, we must also point out that much more than price is considered when selecting suppliers. Other factors, such as on-time delivery, product quality, and the ability of the supplier to ramp up quickly to meet periods of high demand, may be equally or more important than pricing, in which case throughput analysis becomes only a secondary factor in the supplier selection decision.

COST REPORTING

One of the chief problems created by the accountant in relation to constraint management is the reporting of product costs. Accountants are trained to report product costs based on generally accepted accounting principles (GAAP), which require that overhead costs be charged to inventory. The problem is that most of these overhead expenses have no direct bearing on the production of each incremental unit of production, and inflate the cost of each unit of production— frequently by several orders of magnitude beyond the cost of the variable components of a product.

When managers use the fully burdened cost of a product to make decisions in such areas as pricing and product cancellation, the added overhead cost frequently results in incorrect incremental decisions. For example, if a company's product has a totally variable cost of $1 and a fully burdened cost of $3, and a customer requests a one-time price of $2, then the request would normally be rejected out of hand, because the fully burdened cost exceeds the proposed price. In reality, the offer will generate some throughput, since the price exceeds the product's totally variable cost. Consequently, management should at least consider the offer, judging it in relation to the throughput generated by other products (and as described throughout Chapter 4, Throughput and Financial Analysis Scenarios).

So what is the accountant to do? The best solution is to calculate one set of costs for GAAP reporting purposes, and another set of costs that are to be used for throughput analysis. Since the differences between these two costs are likely to be substantial, the accountant should completely segregate the GAAP costs from management in order to avoid confusion, and use them only within the accounting department when financial statements must be constructed.

STAFFING DECISIONS

A key problem in throughput analysis is the determination of when to hire more employees, for the model focuses most on the matching of demand and capacity, rather than permanent changes in staffing levels.

The primary criterion for a staffing increase at locations upstream from the constrained resource is to hire when the company requires long periods of time to recover from production shortfalls, when inventory buffers are so small that they are repeatedly penetrated, and when these problems can be resolved by adding staff to upstream work centers.

The situation is simplified at the constraint, where it is always acceptable to add staff as long as their incremental cost is lower than any throughput increase resulting from their addition.

THE PROBLEM WITH USING THROUGHPUT ACCOUNTING FOR TACTICAL CHANGES

There is a danger in using throughput accounting to prioritize customer orders after they have already arrived in house. If company management is knowledgeable in throughput analysis, it may use this knowledge to delay low-throughput customer orders in order to achieve higher short-term profitability. The obvious problem is that some orders could be delayed well beyond their original promise dates, which may result in customers shifting their future orders to more reliable suppliers. Taken to an extreme, this approach can result in orders being continually driven to the bottom of the production priority list until such time as the mix of existing orders creates an opening at the constrained resource that allows it to be produced (which may result in some orders *never* being shipped). In addition, this action merely shifts low-throughput orders into a later reporting period, where the company will now be more likely to experience even lower throughput due to the presence of an increasing volume of low-throughput orders in its production backlog.

The obvious solution is to completely separate throughput analysis from the production scheduling function. The scheduling staff should be confined to the already-complex task of scheduling the production of all customer orders that have been received, without even knowing what the throughput of various orders may be. This will result in a reasonable mix of orders being delivered that have a full range of throughput dollars associated with each one. Thus, throughput analysis should not be used at the tactical level of scheduling production.

A better level of planning using throughput analysis is at the strategic level, where the company decides whether it will produce low-throughput products at all, before they are even offered for sale to customers. Once they are offered for sale, it is now too late to use throughput analysis, unless it involves changes in pricing (as described in Chapter 4, Throughput and Financial Analysis Scenarios).

It is also useful to use throughput analysis as part of the target costing system. Under target costing, a product design team determines the price point at which a prospective new product can be sold, and then designs a product to have a cost that will generate a sufficient profit at the predetermined price point. Throughput analysis can yield valuable information by eliminating any nonvariable costs assigned to a new product, so that management can determine the true throughput contribution of the product.

In short, throughput analysis is most useful for creating a mix of products that creates the highest possible level of throughput, but should not be used to prioritize product deliveries once the company has committed itself to shipping them.

THROUGHPUT SOFTWARE AND MAKESHIFT SYSTEMS

It is difficult to locate software that assists in throughput analysis because it requires the integration of disparate data—sales data and product costs (i.e., transaction data) from the accounting system, and bills of material, routings, and equipment lists (i.e., master data) from the materials planning system. One company that has achieved this integration is pVelocity, Inc. (located on the Internet at www.pvelocity.com). It sells MPI (Manufacturing Profit Intelligence) software, which collects both master data and transaction data, and assembles it to derive profits and conduct "what if" analyses by customer, order, product, market segments, or product groups. To date, the software is designed for the chemicals, extrusion, and consumer packaged goods industries. Unfortunately, the MPI software is expensive and requires significant installation time, because it must interface with a broad array of in-house databases.

Is it really necessary to reconfigure existing systems to arrive at a throughput system? For smaller companies with simplified product lines, spreadsheet analysis is sufficient, though greater degrees of system complexity, with multiple product lines and equipment routings, will call for the use of more formal systems.

If a company's operations are relatively simple, only a few ingredients are needed to create an adequate throughput analysis system:

1. *Product prices and variable costs.* This information is readily available from most accounting systems. If there is no formal bill of materials, then the cost accountant must summarize variable cost information from supplier invoices. The accountant can then compile this information into a total throughput by product table.

2. *Capacity usage information.* If the company has bill of material or routing information, the accountant can extract from it the amount of time required by each product at the constrained resource. The accountant then divides this usage information into the total throughput figures obtained in the first step to arrive at throughput per minute of constraint time for each product.

3. *Capacity information.* The final ingredient for the in-house throughput analysis system is information about the average available amount of capacity for the constrained resource, stated in minutes. This can be obtained from a work center usage report, or by having the industrial engineering staff compile the information. By adding the available constraint time to the total throughput by product table, we arrive at the throughput decision table used so extensively in Chapter 4, Throughput and Financial Analysis Scenarios.

An example of how to construct a throughput analysis model is provided in Chapter 10, Throughput Case Studies.

SUMMARY

This chapter has shown that the accountant can use throughput accounting to assist with a broad array of decision areas. These include the proper allocation of resources, how inventory levels should be matched to available capacity, when to build inventory, when funds should be invested in capital purchases, how to formulate prices, what types of product costs to report to management, and when to hire additional staff. Of particular importance is when *not* to use throughput accounting, since it is a better tool at the strategic level than for some day-to-day tactical decisions.

We now move to Chapter 10, which is comprised of a series of case studies that use the concepts described thus far to show how throughput accounting can be used in practice.

10

THROUGHPUT CASE STUDIES

The case studies in this chapter are primarily focused on the operating concepts of constraint management, rather than throughput analysis. This is because throughput analysis examples have already been given in Chapter 4, Throughput and Financial Analysis Scenarios. Case studies covered here are as follows:

Locating the constraint
Managing the constraint
Calculating the constraint buffer size
Calculating the materials release dates
Constructing a throughput analysis model
Outsourcing production
The low-price special deal

CASE STUDY: LOCATING THE CONSTRAINT

The Baroque Furniture Company specializes in the construction and gilding of carved furniture. Its production manager has just returned from a constraint management seminar, and wants to locate the constraint within Baroque's production process. Baroque uses the following steps to create its signature line of gilded furniture:

1. Assemble furniture kits from subcontractor
2. Hand carve designs on furniture
3. Add a calcium carbonate and adhesive base layer to the furniture
4. Apply pigment to adhesive base layer
5. Apply gold leaf
6. Burnish gold leaf

Baroque's production policies have thus far emphasized high levels of efficiency for all production processes, so an examination of work center utilization levels only reveals that *all* parts of the production process are being heavily used.

Another way to locate the constraint is to determine which processes have the largest build-up of work-in-process inventory in front of them, which implies that they have insufficient capacity to handle the standard workload. The production manager obtains the backlog information shown in Exhibit 10.1, which itemizes the total minutes of processing time required to clear the backlog in front of each workstation:

The exhibit reveals that Baroque appears to have *two* constrained resources, which are the wood carving and burnishing departments. Both have large work backlogs of approximately the same size.

The production manager now has the opportunity to select which of the two processes will be the primary production constraint. Both departments require large quantities of manual labor to complete, so Baroque can hire additional staff or internally shift staff between workstations to reduce the backlog in both areas. However, the burnishing process requires minimal skill, whereas the wood carving process requires very expensive labor, which is also hard to attract and retain. Accordingly, the production manager shifts several employees from the furniture assembly area to the gold leaf burnishing department, resulting in the modified work backlog shown in Exhibit 10.2, where 1,000 minutes of work backlog has been added to the furniture

Step	Process	Minutes to Process Backlog
1	Assemble furniture kits from subcontractor	895
2	Hand carve designs on furniture	3,050
3	Add adhesive base layer	290
4	Apply pigment to adhesive base layer	510
5	Apply gold leaf	1,400
6	Burnish gold leaf	3,425

EXHIBIT 10.1 WORK BACKLOG FOR EACH WORK STATION

Step	Process	Minutes to Process Backlog
1	Assemble furniture kits from subcontractor	1,895
2	Hand carve designs on furniture	3,050
3	Add adhesive base layer	290
4	Apply pigment to adhesive base layer	510
5	Apply gold leaf	1,400
6	Burnish gold leaf	2,425

EXHIBIT 10.2 MODIFIED WORK BACKLOG FOR EACH WORK STATION

assembly area (because its staffing has been reduced) and 1,000 minutes of backlog have been cut from the burnishing area (because its staffing has been increased).

By shifting some low-skilled labor between work areas, the production manager has clearly identified the wood carving department as being Baroque's preferred choice for its constrained resource. Baroque can now focus on the management of this high labor-cost area, as is described in the next case study.

CASE STUDY: MANAGING THE CONSTRAINT

In the preceding case study, the Baroque Furniture Company (Baroque) has chosen its wood carving process to be its constrained resource. This is an excellent choice of constraint, because of the high cost of the skilled labor needed for the wood carving process. Baroque's production manager, Mr. Stark, finds that this work area currently has a backlog of 3,050 minutes of work. At an average throughput per minute of $8.00 or $480.00 per hour, this represents $24,400 of throughput that Baroque is unable to recognize.

Due to the highly individual nature of the work, Mr. Stark finds that it is not feasible to cover employee break time or lost time that occurs at shift changes; it is simply impossible to have more than one person carve a single piece of furniture. However, further analysis reveals that the wood carvers divide their work into two stages, which is the tracing of their proposed design on the furniture, followed by carving in multiple stages to attain the proper level of relief. Mr. Stark finds that, by hiring lower-cost artisans who first trace designs onto the wood surfaces of the furniture, the carvers can concentrate their attention strictly on the carving work, resulting in a higher level of capacity.

Mr. Stark now divides the wood carving department into two departments, the first being for design tracing and the second for wood carving. By more narrowly defining the scope of the constrained resource, the same group of wood carvers now has extra time to devote to carving, which results in a drop in the number of backlog minutes.

Mr. Stark also discovers that an occasional piece of furniture develops cracks that are only discovered during the gilding stage, when the gold lamination tends to highlight irregularities in the underlying material. This problem applies to only 1 percent of all furniture pieces used, but this means that it wastes 1 percent of the throughput of the wood carving operation, since the results of its efforts must now be scrapped. Stark finds that it is possible to discover these flaws with a high degree of accuracy simply by scanning the wood with a small magnifying lens, called a hand loupe. Since the new design tracing team positioned immediately in front of the carving department has excess time available, he arranges to have them conduct the quality assurance review with hand loupes. By doing so, Baroque incurs no additional labor expenditure and only a tiny investment in hand loupes, and effectively increases the throughput of the carving operation by 1 percent.

Mr. Stark also finds that an excessive degree of burnishing in the last production step can heat the underlying wood surface to such an extent that the gold surface becomes discolored. When this happens, all gilding must be removed, the wood surface sanded down by the wood carving department, and the gilding reapplied. In the most recent month, this rework required 550 minutes of work by the wood carvers. At $8 per minute of throughput time, this represented the loss of $4,400 of throughput. However, by positioning thermal sensors near the wood surfaces during the burnishing stage, employees could be warned of temperature increases likely to cause discoloration, and stop burnishing until temperature levels drop. Buy purchasing ten of these thermal sensors for $250 each, Mr. Stark can invest $2,500 and earn back his investment in saved throughput in just a few weeks.

By shifting some tasks away from the constrained resource, moving the quality assurance function immediately in front of the constraint, and reducing rework, Baroque has increased the amount of throughput generated by its furniture wood carving department, without adding any expensive staff to this operation.

CASE STUDY: CALCULATING THE CONSTRAINT BUFFER SIZE

In the preceding two case studies, the Baroque Furniture Company (Baroque) has chosen its wood carving department to be its constrained resource, and has taken a number of steps to improve the throughput of that operation. Another problem faced by Baroque is its furniture source, which is located in Italy. For highly precise wood carving, the best wood choice is Italian walnut, which Baroque purchases from the Lombardy region of north-central Italy. The supplier processes the wood into pre-cut furniture kits, which Baroque's assembly operation drills and glues together before passing them along to the wood carving department. Because of the distant location of its furniture source, Baroque has historically taken advantage of large shipping container sizes and ordered in bulk, thereby reducing its shipping costs. However, this also means that replenishment deliveries only arrive at long intervals, which increases the risk that a materials shortage may occur that would shut down the wood carving department.

The production manager, Mr. Stark, faces the alternatives of doing nothing, placing smaller furniture orders that are delivered more frequently, or creating an inventory buffer to protect the wood carving department from materials shortages. An evaluation of each alternative reveals the following:

1. *Do nothing.* A review of stockout conditions at the wood carving department reveals that the department averages 500 minutes of downtime per month that is caused by materials shortages. At an average throughput rate of $8.00 per minute, this equates to $4,000 per month of lost throughput (500 minutes of downtime × $8.00/minute average throughput). Thus, Baroque would lose $4,000 per month by taking no action.

2. *Place smaller orders.* If Baroque places orders of half the usual size and does so twice as frequently, then the duration of the average stockout period should be cut in half, which reduces the minutes of downtime per month by half, to 250. This equates to a reduction of lost throughput of $2,000 (250 minutes downtime saved × $8.00/minute average throughput). However, because furniture is now shipped in smaller quantities, freight charges increase by $1,750 per month, resulting in a net profit improvement of only $250 per month.

3. *Create inventory buffer.* Mr. Stark calculates that if Baroque invests in an inventory buffer costing $10,000, this will be of a size sufficient to prevent 300 minutes of downtime per month that would otherwise be caused by material shortages. To eliminate the entire 500 minutes

of downtime caused by material shortages will require a much larger inventory buffer of $40,000. In the first case, increased throughput of $2,400 per month (300 minutes × $8.00/minute average throughput) equates to a payback period of the $10,000 investment of about four months. In the second case, increased throughput of $4,000 per month (500 minutes × $8.00/minute average throughput) equates to a payback period of the $40,000 investment of about ten months.

Of the scenarios presented, Mr. Stark would be well advised to build a $40,000 inventory buffer in front of the wood carving department, thereby earning a significant return on this working capital investment within one year.

CASE STUDY: CALCULATING THE MATERIALS RELEASE DATES

As noted in the preceding three case studies, the Baroque Furniture Company constructs furniture from kits delivered from its Italian supplier, carves ornate patterns in the furniture, and applies gilding to the results before shipping them to customers. Baroque's production manager, Mr. Stark, is having problems determining the precise point in time when furniture kits should be released from the warehouse into the furniture assembly department, which in turn feeds the constrained resource, which is the wood carving department. There is some pressure from the sales staff to tell Baroque's demanding customers that their orders are "in production," which means that orders are released into the manufacturing area before they can be processed. By doing so, the furniture assembly department becomes flooded with work-in-process, making it difficult to determine which jobs are to be completed next.

During a seminar on constraint management, Mr. Stark learns that materials should be released based on the processing time required by all operations upstream of the constrained resource, while still ensuring that the inventory buffer in front of the constraint remains full. Since there is only one depart-ment upstream of the wood carving department (i.e., the furniture assembly department), the release of materials into the production area is calculated based on the time required to assemble each furniture model. There is no batching policy requiring several items of furniture to be completed before being transported to the inventory buffer; instead, each completed item is transported to the buffer at once. The furniture department assembles four types of furniture, which are identified in the following table along with their assembly times:

Furniture Type	Assembly Type
Chair, Louis XIV style	9 hours
Console table, duke style	7 hours
Cupboard, imperial style	20 hours
Mini chaise, viscount style	12 hours

Multiple furniture kits of each model are being assembled at any given time. To create a controlled release of materials, Mr. Stark pre-positions a one-day supply of kits in front of the assembly area, and then releases then into that department using a kanban system, whereby the completion of one item of furniture triggers the release of a corresponding kit into the assembly area. For example, there are always five imperial style cupboards being assembled; given a total assembly time of 20 hours each, one cupboard should be completed every four hours. Accordingly, the warehouse staff positions two cupboard kits in front of the assembly area (comprising one day of demand), and moves one into the assembly area every four hours, as soon as a completed unit is sent to the inventory buffer in front of the wood carving department.

The result is a considerable reduction in work-in-process, with more inventory being retained in the warehouse, rather than cluttering the production area.

CASE STUDY: CONSTRUCTING A THROUGHPUT ANALYSIS MODEL

The production manager of the Baroque Furniture Company, Mr. Stark, wants to develop a throughput analysis model that he can use to evaluate a large customer order (as described in the following case study). To do so, he first locates the product price list, which is shown in Exhibit 10.3.

Product Name	Product Price
Cupboard, imperial model	$14,000
Chair, Louis XIV model	4,200
Console table, duke model	5,000
Mini chaise, viscount model	3,600

EXHIBIT 10.3 BAROQUE FURNITURE COMPANY PRICE LIST

Product Name	Product Price	Kit Cost	Kit Shipping	2% Commission	Variable Cost	Throughput
Cupboard, imperial model	$14,000	$4,850	$545	$280	$5,675	$8,325
Chair, Louis XIV model	4,200	1,410	156	84	1,650	2,550
Console table, duke model	5,000	1,580	180	100	1,860	3,140
Mini chaise, viscount model	3,600	1,730	198	72	2,000	1,600

EXHIBIT 10.4 PRODUCT THROUGHPUT CALCULATION

Mr. Stark then determines the totally variable cost associated with each product. Investigation reveals that only the cost of the furniture kits, kit shipping, and the 2 percent salesperson commission can be considered totally variable costs. He loads this information into the table shown in Exhibit 10.4, which includes product prices, to arrive at the throughput dollars per unit.

Next, Mr. Stark uses labor routing records for the wood carving department to determine the number of minutes required to carve each type of furniture. He divides this time by the throughput calculated in Exhibit 10.4 to arrive at the throughput per minute of each product, as shown in Exhibit 10.5.

Mr. Stark then calculates the actual amount of monthly production time available at the constrained resource (e.g., the wood carving department).

Product Name	Throughput	Total Minutes at the Constraint	Throughput/ Minute of Constraint
Cupboard, imperial model	$8,325	900	$9.25
Chair, Louis XIV model	2,550	300	8.50
Console table, duke model	3,140	400	7.85
Mini chaise, viscount model	1,600	250	6.40

EXHIBIT 10.5 THROUGHPUT PER MINUTE CALCULATION

He uses the following calculation to arrive at the total number of constraint minutes:

	16	Wood carvers
×	21	Business days per month
×	8	Hours per day
×	60	Minutes per hour
×	0.78125	Percent efficiency
=	126,000	Minutes of maximum constraint time

A last data collection step is to determine the total amount of operating expense incurred by Baroque in an average month, as well as the total invested funds. The total operating expense should be all expenses except the kit cost, kit shipping cost, and 2 percent commission that were already enumerated as

totally variable expenses in Exhibit 10.4. The remaining costs are $1,050,000 per month. The total amount of invested funds is $3,625,000, which is comprised of Baroque's investment in working capital and fixed assets.

Finally, Mr. Stark assembles the information compiled in the preceding steps to construct the throughput analysis model shown in Exhibit 10.6.

Note that the sequence of products listed in the first column of Exhibit 10.6 is in declining order by throughput per minute of constraint time. As explained in Chapter 4, Throughput and Financial Analysis Scenarios, this sort order places the most profitable (i.e., high throughput) products in the top (priority) position for the scheduling of production, with the lowest profitability (i.e., low throughput) products listed at the bottom. In this case, the cupboard is

Product Name	Throughput $/Minute of Constraint	Required Constraint Usage (minutes)	Units of Scheduled Production	Constraint Utilization (minutes)	Throughput per Product
1. Cupboard, imperial	$9.25	900	0/0	0	$ 0
2. Chair, Louis XIV	8.50	300	0/0	0	0
3. Console table, duke	7.85	400	0/0	0	0
4. Mini chaise, viscount	6.40	250	0/0	0	0
		Total planned constraint time	0		—
		Maximum constraint time	126,000		—
		Throughput total		$	0
		Operating expense total		1,050,000	
		Profit		$	0
		Profit percentage			%
		Investment		$3,625,000	
		Return on investment*			%

*Annualized

EXHIBIT 10.6 THROUGHPUT PER MINUTE CALCULATION

the most profitable and the mini chaise the least profitable. Mr. Stark is now ready to use the throughput analysis model, which occurs in the following case study.

CASE STUDY: OUTSOURCING PRODUCTION

The Baroque Furniture Company has received an order from the Association of Teutonic Castles (ATC) to refurnish a large number of its castle theme parks in northern Germany with baroque furniture. The furniture must be delivered by a specific date, or else the entire order will be canceled. The order is larger than Baroque's current capacity is designed to handle. The initial throughput model for a one-month period, including the ATC order, is shown in Exhibit 10.7.

The model shows that, though Baroque would earn an all-time high monthly profit of $88,500 (as opposed to its usual $40,000 monthly profit), it is unable to fulfill the entire ATC order, as it only has enough capacity to build the cupboards and chairs, but not the console tables or mini chaises. These two additional items require an additional 54,500 minutes of constraint time, which is calculated as follows:

Furniture Model	Units Needed	Constraint Time/Unit	Total Time Needed
Console table, duke model	80	400 minutes	32,000 minutes
Mini chaise, viscount model	90	250 minutes	22,500 minutes
Totals	170		54,500 minutes

Product Name	Throughput $/Minute of Constraint	Required Constraint Usage (minutes)	Units of Scheduled Production	Constraint Utilization (minutes)	Throughput per Product
1. Cupboard, imperial	$9.25	900	100/100	90,000	$ 832,500
2. Chair, Louis XIV	8.50	300	120/120	36,000	306,000
3. Console table, duke	7.85	400	0/80	N/A	0
4. Mini chaise, viscount	6.40	250	0/90	N/A	0
		Total planned constraint time		126,000	—
		Maximum constraint time		126,000	—
			Throughput total		$1,138,500
			Operating expense total		1,050,000
			Profit		$ 88,500
			Profit percentage		7.7%
			Investment		$3,625,000
			Return on investment*		29.3%

*Annualized

EXHIBIT 10.7 INITIAL THROUGHPUT MODEL FOR THE BAROQUE FURNITURE COMPANY

Before rejecting the order, the company first explores the possibility of out-sourcing production of the console table and mini chaise to a subcontractor, Rococo Designs Group, by shipping assembled furniture to them for all wood carving work, and then having them returned for all remaining production steps.

If Baroque could complete the console tables in-house, it would earn through-put per unit of $3,140 ($7.85 throughput per minute × 400 minutes of constraint time, as noted in Exhibit 10.7), while it could earn throughput per unit of $1,600 ($6.40 per minute × 250 minutes of constraint time, as noted in Exhibit 10.7) if it could complete the mini chaises in-house. Rococo quotes a price of $3,250 per unit for the console tables and $2,000 per unit for the mini chaises. These prices eliminate all throughput that Baroque could have earned from the sale of these items. However, before rejecting the Rococo bid, it is necessary to enter the bid information in a revised throughput model to determine the outcome of the order on the entire production system, as shown in Exhibit 10.8.

Exhibit 10.8 reveals that Baroque will still earn a profit of $43,540, which is higher than its usual monthly profit of $40,000, if it accepts the ATC order. Though it will lose money by outsourcing work on two products, the incremental increase in profits on two other products results in an acceptable level of profit for the entire ATC order.

Product Name	Throughput $/Minute of Constraint	Required Constraint Usage (minutes)	Units of Scheduled Production	Constraint Utilization (minutes)	Throughput per Product
1. Cupboard, imperial	$9.25	900	100/100	90,000	$ 832,500
2. Chair, Louis XIV	8.50	300	120/120	36,000	306,000
3. Console table, duke	−0.28	400	80/80	N/A	(8,960)
4. Mini chaise, viscount	−1.60	250	90/90	N/A	(36,000)
		Total planned constraint time		126,000	—
		Maximum constraint time		126,000	—
				Throughput total	$1,093,540
				Operating expense total	1,050,000
				Profit	$ 43,540
				Profit percentage	4.0%
				Investment	$3,625,000
				Return on investment*	14.4%

*Annualized

EXHIBIT 10.8 REVISED THROUGHPUT MODEL FOR THE BAROQUE FURNITURE COMPANY

CASE STUDY: THE LOW-PRICE SPECIAL DEAL

Savile Row Tailors creates small quantities of men's suits at its factory in London, all made to a standard pattern, which are then sold to high-end retail chains throughout the world. Savile produces suits using multiple fabrics, as well as one traditional shooting suit for outdoor use, which are outlined in the throughput model shown in Exhibit 10.9. The constrained resource is the sewing operation, which runs for two shifts per day, an average of 21 business days per month, at 80 percent efficiency, or 16,128 minutes per month (16 hours × 60 minutes/hour × 21 days × 80 percent). The time required to make each suit is essentially identical, with the primary difference in throughput being the cost of the fabric. Only the shooting suit requires extra constraint usage, due to the additional number of suit pockets. Due to constraint limitations, Savile is unable to fulfill the monthly demand of 75 shooting suits; it is currently able to complete 48 of these suits per month.

Savile is approached by the purchasing manager of Dilway, a large American clothier, to create for it a branded boutique line of silk suits to be called the J.J. Weatherley line. Dilway is willing to guarantee a minimum production volume of 50 suits per month for the first year, but only if Savile agrees to what amounts to an 8 percent drop in throughput from its current silk suit, while using the same quality of silk materials used in its own suit. Thus, Savile cannot recover any profits from cost reductions, and must instead accept a lower level of throughput per suit produced. If Savile were to accept this proposal, the J.J. Weatherly suit would have a throughput of $3.86 per minute of constraint time, which slightly exceeds the throughput that Savile currently obtains from its shooting suit. The impact on the throughput model is shown in Exhibit 10.10.

As a comparison of the initial and revised throughput models show, there is a negligible impact on throughput, profits, or return on investment, though the company will be unable to manufacture more than a few shooting suits. In this case, Savile must make the order acceptance decision based on other factors than throughput. One factor is that the shooting suit market has been a long-term one with a steady clientele, and so provides enough throughput to ensure that the company turns a profit every year. Dilway, however, is a new customer with a large distribution channel, and so presents the prospect for greater sales volume over time, if Savile is willing to add capacity to accommodate future orders. Thus, the decision hinges upon the offsetting factors of losing a steady source of throughput (shooting suits) in exchange for a potentially large new customer (Dilway). The second factor is only relevant if Savile can add capacity easily to accommodate more suit orders from Dilway. If not, then Savile would be more likely to either reject the order or to issue a counterproposal for a higher price per suit.

Product Name	Throughput $/Minute of Constraint	Required Constraint Usage (minutes)	Units of Scheduled Production	Constraint Utilization (minutes)	Throughput per Product
1. High twist wool suit	$5.55	90	40/40	3,600	$ 19,980
2. Skill suit	4.20	90	50/50	4,500	18,900
3. Mohair suit	3.90	90	30/30	2,700	10,530
4. Tweed shooting suit	3.85	110	48/75	5,280	20,328
		Total planned constraint time		**16,080**	—
		Maximum constraint time		**16,128**	—
			Throughput total		**$ 69,738**
			Operating expense total		60,500
			Profit		$9,238
			Profit percentage		13.2%
			Investment		$450,000
			Return on investment*		24.6%

*Annualized

EXHIBIT 10.9   INITIAL THROUGHPUT MODEL FOR THE SAVILE ROW TAILORS

Product Name	Throughput $/Minute of Constraint	Required Constraint Usage (minutes)	Units of Scheduled Production	Constraint Utilization (minutes)	Throughput per Product
1. High twist wool suit	$5.55	90	40/40	3,600	$ 19,980
2. Skill suit	4.20	90	50/50	4,500	18,900
3. Mohair suit	3.90	90	30/30	2,700	10,530
4. J.J. Weatherly suit	3.86	90	50/50	4,500	17,370
5. Tweed shooting suit	3.85	110	7/75	770	2,965
		Total planned constraint time		**16,070**	—
		Maximum constraint time		**16,128**	—
			Throughput total		**$ 69,745**
			Operating expense total		60,500
			Profit		$9,245
			Profit percentage		13.2%
			Investment		$450,000
			Return on investment*		24.7%

*Annualized

EXHIBIT 10.10   REVISED THROUGHPUT MODEL FOR THE SAVILE ROW TAILORS

SUMMARY

This chapter has listed a number of case studies showing key concepts of constraint management and throughput accounting, including locating and managing the constraint, how to determine materials release dates, how to create a throughput analysis model, and when to outsource production. Though these case studies are necessarily simplistic in comparison to the great complexity of most corporate systems, they show the general outlines of how constraint-related issues can be investigated and resolved. As was the case for much of this book, the case studies are intended to provide general direction, which the reader can then apply to real-world situations.

INDEX